BIRDS
of
SINGAPORE

Birds of Singapore
Edited by Jane Perkins

© 1987 Times Editions Pte Ltd
Times Centre, 1 New Industrial Road
Singapore 1953

Times Subang
Lot 46, Subang Hi-Tech Industrial Park
Batu Tiga, 40000 Shah Alam
Selangor Darul Ehsan, Malaysia

First published 1987
Reprinted 1988, 1990, 1995

Typeset by Superskill, Singapore
Colour separation by Daiichi, Singapore
Printed by Welpac Printing & Packaging Pte Ltd

ISBN 981 204 576 7

BIRDS

of

SINGAPORE

by

Christopher Hails

Illustrated by

Frank Jarvis

TIMES EDITIONS

CONTENTS

FOREWORD

It has been said that a mark of civilisation is the importance which its people give to wild creatures. Development which shows no regard for them cannot be considered civilised development. Our planet is a living world and we are simply a small, but disproportionally destructive, part of it. Unless man can learn to live in harmony with his environment, the destruction of his natural heritage will demean his material achievements.

Developing the resources of a country without destroying the environment is not an impossible achievement for those who are motivated, but it requires a willingness to make minor sacrifices and above all a great deal of knowledge, not only of the techniques of development but of the functioning of the environment and the requirements of wild organisms. Once sufficient experience in both areas of knowledge has been acquired, then the two must be moulded skilfully together.

This book marks a first step in the process, by advancing and disseminating knowledge about an important group of wild animals. In safeguarding and conserving our environment, education is of prime importance. Environmental awareness by the general public and the cultivation of a taste in the natural world must be given high priority: the more people who learn and understand the beauty and wonder of nature, the more there will be who wish to protect rather than destroy it.

It is a sad fact of life that those who have the power to control the fate of the living world, are often the least well informed about it. With this book it will be possible for even the busiest of people to achieve a useful level of expertise, by devoting a small amount of time to its pages. The tropical regions of the world are badly in need of such texts, since they are the areas which contain the greatest wealth of wildlife and stand to benefit most by having a public which is fully aware of the importance of conserving its natural heritage.

We must set our goals to ensure that an appreciation of nature will grow alongside all other aspects of human development.

Sir Peter Scott
Gloucester England
Honorary Chairman of the World Wildlife Fund
International Council

July, 1986

PREFACE

The aim of this book is to act as a stimulus for those people who have a new or casual interest in birds, and wish to learn more or simply satisfy a passing curiosity. We hope that it will also serve the newcomer or visitor, both as an introduction to the more common birds and a guide to where they are most likely to be found.

The biggest problem confronting any newcomer to the art of birdwatching is how to correctly identify the species they have seen. To this end there is nothing which can compare with an accurate colour illustration showing the bird's important characteristics.

Having made an attempt at an identification the next objective is to try and find out a little more about what it is, what it does, and perhaps why. The answer to some of these questions can also help to confirm or refute an identification, by checking if the habitat in which the bird was seen is common and appropriate or if its behaviour fits the characteristic pattern of the species.

So our objective in this book is to combine colour illustrations of the birds, in postures which reflect their behaviour in the wild, with a text which conveys something of what is known of their habits and distribution in Singa-

pore. The latter is increasingly important because the face of Singapore has changed dramatically over the last two decades and bird distributions have been found to have altered accordingly.

Not all the species found in Singapore are covered. To have done so would have left little space for the text, resulting in a field guide containing a thorough coverage of species but conveying considerably less information.

In our experience the people with only a casual interest, or those new to the world of birds, are more often confused and deterred when confronted by the apparent range of species to be recognised. Thus, by limiting the coverage to those species most likely to be seen, we hope the book will serve as an introduction for the newcomer, and thereby stimulate more people to join the ever-growing band of serious birdwatchers in Singapore.

The choice of species will undoubtedly invite criticism. We have included all those species which the casual observer has a good chance of encountering. On some occasions less common species are included because they are related to more common species in some interesting way, or because their status is undergoing some sort of change. For many of them our knowledge is still very scant. Hopefully we are laying the foundation for more systematic observations, resulting in more substantial books in the future.

For the serious birdwatcher, who has already achieved a certain level of competence, a very thorough field guide (King, Woodcock and Dickinson) already exists which will help identify all the species found in South-east Asia. For this group we have included chapters on the ecology of birds in Singapore and as much detail of their behaviour and habits as space will permit. In this way we hope to encourage people to learn more about the birds rather than just collecting the names of species seen.

We also include a checklist of those species found in Singapore and their status. By using this list any reader can go to more comprehensive texts to check on species not covered in this book.

ACKNOWLEDGEMENTS

We would not have been able to complete this work without the help and advice of many people. Chris Hails would especially like to thank David Wells, for his expert guidance and help rendered at every stage of the project. Also David Bradford, Hugh Buck and Richard Ollington, who provided his first introduction to birding in Singapore. Substantial parts of the text were read and improved by David Bryant, Hugh Buck, David Waugh and David Wells. Richard Corlett and Jon Sigurdsson provided expert opinions on aspects of Singapore's ecology. Ching Kok Ann helped with numerous tasks.

Frank Jarvis wishes to make special thanks to J.R.C. Ironside for both moral and material support throughout the project. To Victor Mason for first stimulating his interest in South-east Asian birds; and to Leo Haks and Duncan Parrish for help in other ways.

We both thank Mrs Yang Chang Man for her help whilst working with the National University of Singapore Zoological Reference Collection, and Kang Nee and Morten Strange for the use of photographs.

Most important of all was the patience, support and self-sacrifice provided by our wives. In particular Jane Jarvis provided her own botanical artwork as reference material for plants in the plates, and Sandra Hails read and greatly improved the entire text and provided numerous valuable opinions throughout the project.

To all these people we give our unreserved thanks, fully realising that the errors and shortcomings of the final version are entirely of our own making.

C.J. Hails, Singapore
F. Jarvis, Scotland   June 1986

WHEN SMALL IS RICH

At first sight the Republic's statistics would not suggest an island with much to offer the wildlife enthusiast. Singapore consists of one main island and about 30 smaller ones, the latter being found mostly to the south. In total the land area is only about 620 km². The main island is 40 km at its widest point and 22 km at its greatest depth. At the time of writing it is home to slightly more than 2.5 million people and consequently has large housing and industrial estates scattered around it in a series of small towns.

However, as far as birds are concerned, we have a list of almost 300 species which have been seen here in recent years (see Checklist). This degree of richness in such a small island is due to a mixture of circumstances.

The major factor is the location of Singapore at latitude 1°20″ north, only 135 km north of the equator. This position, in the heart of the tropical belt, means that the temperature is hot throughout the year with a daily average of 26.6°C, the difference between the hottest and coolest month of the

year is only 2°C whilst the daily fluctuation is 7°C. It is also wet with 2,400 mm of rain spread fairly evenly thoughout the year. As if to reinforce the constancy of the climate annual changes in day-length are limited to only nine minutes. Buffering Singapore against any small climatic changes which may occur under these conditions is the sea, which totally surrounds the island. The sea temperature is a constant 28°C and there are no cold currents to bring any changes in the temperature.

These continuous hot, moist conditions give rise to luxuriant natural vegetation. Until the hand of man altered things drastically Singapore was cloaked in a layer of tropical rainforest with mangroves around the coastline. Tropical rainforest is biologically the most diverse habitat in the world. In it we can find more species of plants and animals per unit area than in any other habitat. In this respect the forests of Singapore would have had much in common with those in neighbouring Malaysia and Indonesia.

However, being a small island the variety of forest habitats, and therefore the variety of bird species, has always been less than in these adjacent countries. For ex-

The island which forms the main landmass of Singapore is a mosaic of green areas and urban development (photo: Ian Lloyd).

11

ample the highest point in Singapore is Bukit Timah Nature Reserve which is only 165m above sea level. Thus there are no montane bird species. It is also an established ecological phenomenon that small islands hold fewer species of animals than equivalent areas of nearby mainlands (partly for the reason cited above), and that the physical constraints mean that wildlife populations are more unstable and species extinction is likely to occur more quickly. For these reasons Singapore has never had as rich an avifauna as that found in the lowland forests on the nearby large land masses.

Another feature contributing to the number of bird species found in Singapore is the annual influx of migrants which arrive each year from the north. These are birds which live the middle months of the year in the subtropical and temperate regions of central and northern Asia. There they exploit the brief explosion of food which occurs in the summer.

However, once summer is over, many plants and animals enter a dormant state to survive the cold conditions of winter, food becomes scarce for the birds and so many of them move south before this happens to be assured of a food supply. Starting about September we find an influx of these visitors from the north who stay until March or April when they return north to breed again.

So nature dictated the initial characteristics of the Singapore avifauna in terms of those resident birds of the forests and returning migrants. These characteristics were soon modified by man.

Raffles established the first trading post in 1819 and soon after there followed a period of forest removal to establish crops and settlements. As parcels of land were worked out, new areas were opened up. So systematic was this destruction of natural habitats that by 1859 there were 18,000 ha of abandoned land on the island, mostly covered in grass. At this time most of the forest birds must have retreated into any small remaining pockets, and we have no real idea how many became extinct. The only area to avoid this was the hill at Bukit Timah, our only remnant of those original forests.

In the meantime water storage reservoirs were built for the rapidly-expanding population. They were located in the centre of the island and the land surrounding them was defined as a water catch-

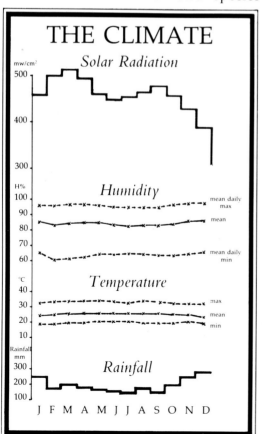

THE CLIMATE

Solar Radiation

mw/cm²
500
400
300

Humidity

H%
100   mean daily max
90
80   mean
70
60   mean daily min

Temperature

°C
40
30   max
20   mean
10   min

Rainfall mm
300
200
100

J F M A M J J A S O N D

ment area. In 1951 the Nature Reserves Ordinance joined the water catchment area and Bukit Timah Hill as a Nature Reserve. Since that time the 2,000 ha central catchment area has re-established itself as tall secondary forest and the surviving forest birds have spread into the regenerating forest.

So the forest, which was the major natural bird habitat, was greatly modified by man. Another important bird habitat, again soon to be modified, was the coastline, the interface of the land and the sea. In Singapore we can divide coastlines into those on sandy shores and those on muddy shores. Mangrove formed the bulk of the vegetation on muddy shores; these were worked for charcoal and construction timbers and large areas of them cleared for prawn farming. More recently the trend has been to reclaim all the shallow water coastal areas for development purposes. The sandy areas from Changi peninsula southwards have all been formed by reclamation works.

Between the coasts and the remaining forest most of the land can be classed as open country, a mosaic comprising the city and its conurbations in the south, and parks, gardens and agricultural land in the north. Of these the agricultural land is the richest in bird life. Unfortunately agriculture is being phased out in Singapore as it occupies much land more urgently required for housing and industrial development.

Not surprisingly these alterations to the physiography of Singapore have brought with them changes in the avifauna. Since records began we have recorded 394 species of birds in Singapore. But so dynamic has been the situation that, at any one point in time, the "currently occurring" list has probably never exceeded 300. Extinction of species due to habitat removal has almost been balanced by invasions of new species and establishment of feral (escaped) species. So the total number of species found in Singapore has only declined by about 13 per cent over the last 80 years or so.

Turnover has been much greater than this, however, and we have lost about 30 percent of those species which occurred here at the turn of the century. Of the 106 species which have been lost, 87 (82 percent) were associated with forest or heavily wooded areas. Total losses include pheasants and hornbills, with considerable reductions in the numbers of species of babblers, woodpeckers, cuckoo-shrikes and bulbuls.

Most of the species which have been lost have not been replaced ecologically by new ones, i.e. the incoming species have not taken over the role of those which became extinct. Of the "new" species 78 percent are of migrant or vagrant status and so their life in Singapore is only transient. Of the permanent additions all are birds which live in the newly-created open country habitats; none have entered the forest.

Comparisons with old lists are complicated by improvement in observer skills and equipment; some of the very rare or vagrant species we now record for the "first" time may have been here before, but escaped notice.

Compared with the past the Singapore of today contains a greater variety of habitats than at any time in history. But most of the habitats that we now have are severely depleted or are far inferior to that which existed before man took a hand in matters.

WHERE THE BIRDS ARE

THE CITY

Many people would raise their eyebrows at the thought of looking for birds in the city area. But the astute observer will be able to find something of interest. In the city every bird must be observed closely as it is too easy to dismiss them as mynas, sparrows or pigeons. I found the first Chinese Crested Myna on the main island in Bras Basah, and have had my finest views of a Peregrine Falcon perching on the radio masts at Fort Canning Park. Oddities like these constitute a red-letter day for the city birder but there is still much interest to be had by closely observing the more common urban species.

City birdwatching can also provide certain food for thought. I wish to stress this point because, although the city birdlife may not be spectacular, it still affords the opportunity to observe and think about the important features of a bird's lifestyle. For example, watch the White-vented Mynas and see how they can switch from scavenging around dustbins to

Rainforest is the exceedingly rich climax habitat of the region, forest birds cannot survive in other habitats (photo: Ian Lloyd).

picking up ants and earthworms on a lawn after rain. They are able to find food in the most unlikely places — drains, roofs, gutters etc. Think how many more rats and cockroaches we would have if they did not have to compete with the mynas for their food. Mynas pair for life and in the breeding season the couple will display to each other by raising the crest and bowing the head up and down. Keep a watch at dusk as the night-time roosts begin to form and birds fly off to join them. Scientists still do not understand the reason for this behaviour.

Look at the Tree Sparrows which can feed literally between our feet and nest in any available nook or cranny. This bird is a relatively shy woodland creature in Europe and yet behaves completely differently in Asia.

Feral domesticated pigeons ("town pigeons") can be seen in many places. The earliest account of their presence in Singapore was in the 1960's when about 100 were in the vicinity of the Victoria Theatre. They are assumed to have originated from escaped birds sold as food. It attests to the rapid success of this invading species that 20 years later we now have over 100 times the original number. They cause many problems by nesting in roof-spaces and soiling paintwork and equipment with their faeces; on the other hand, many people admire them and they are widely fed by shopkeepers, visitors to temples and picnickers in the parks.

The larger city parks have become small sanctuaries in themselves. Fort Canning is one of the best and the visitor can watch Yellow-vented Bulbuls, Black-naped Orioles, Common Iora, Pink-necked Pigeons and Glossy Starlings with ease. This is also a stronghold of the Coppersmith Barbet which feeds in the fine fig trees when they are in fruit.

Also take a look at the trees which line the rivers and drainage canals. These waterways are the commuter belts of the bird world through which they travel from one refuge to another. Four species of kingfisher can be seen using the waterways — Common, Collared, White-throated and Black-capped. I have even heard that little refugee from the forest, the Flyeater, singing its reedy little song in the fig trees by the Singapore River at Boat Quay.

Remember to look up in the air too. Swifts and swiftlets can always be seen in the heart of the city. Some of the old buildings around Shenton Way house their own colonies of swiftlets. The attic rooms and rambling corridors of these buildings simulate the sea-caves which are the natural nesting sites of swiftlets.

Overhead, Brahminy Kites and White-bellied Sea-eagles can be seen soaring. The kites are particularly common around Kallang Basin and the wharf areas. The Sea-eagles nest on Sentosa and regularly soar over the city. In September/October we record good migration passages of the Honey Buzzard and Japanese Sparrowhawk. These migrating birds of prey will congregate in flocks high over the city using the thermals rising off the hot concrete to gain height in order to glide long distances.

At the right time of year a good place to see these migrating hawks is the ridge at Mount Faber, just a little out of the city. From here I have also watched migrating bee-eaters and swifts passing over. I have only twice seen the Rufous-bellied Eagle in Singapore and both times have been from Mount Faber.

So do not despair if your office is on the 21st floor at Shenton Way: look out of the window and you have the opportunity for eyeball to eyeball contact with a wealth of Singapore birdlife still waiting to be properly documented and understood.

COASTAL HABITATS

The sea-shore is a very narrow but unique area which forms the interface between the land and the sea. The type of habitat it offers to birds can be found in no other place. We can broadly divide the Singapore shorelines into those which are predominantly muddy and those which are sandy; there are a few areas which are rocky but these are very limited in extent. Most of the islands to the south also have fringing coral reefs which provide another special type of bird habitat at low tide, but on many islands these have been reclaimed or destroyed by development.

On muddy shorelines the substrates contain a large amount of organic matter interspersed with inorganic particles. This mixture provides food for a large number

16

of mud-dwelling organisms which have specialised feeding mechanisms to separate the two components using the organic matter as a food source.

The sea surrounding us is a soup of biological organisms, many of them microscopic. When they die their carcasses float about in the water, slowly rotting and sinking until they come in contact with the sea bed. This sinking process occurs more quickly in the calm waters which are characteristically found on sheltered shores and in river estuaries. In these areas the carcasses settle out and form deposits of mud on the sea floor where they are mixed with deposits of silt from the river. On exposed shorelines, where there is much stronger wave action and storms, only the very big, heavier particles can settle out and so we get sandy shorelines formed.

The invertebrate animals which feed on the mud or silt congregate in those areas where the organic content of the mud is high, for that is where there is most food for them. However, if it is too high, and the mud is too fine, their feeding and breathing apparatus becomes clogged. Also oxygen cannot penetrate far into these fine sediments. Thus the invertebrates must compromise and live in those places where the mud is rich, but not too rich. We find that they reach their greatest densities in substrates of intermediate particle size. On the sandy shorelines, where the particle size is largest, there is very little organic matter and therefore far fewer of these invertebrates.

I have gone to some pains to explain the distribution of foreshore invertebrates because these constitute the major food items for those birds which live on the shorelines. So the distribution of the birds matches rather well with the distribution of the invertebrates which in turn are dependent upon the nature of the substrate. The most apparent result of these relationships for the birdwatcher is the large numbers of birds which congregate on muddy foreshores and the relative scarcity of them on sandy shorelines. If we look more closely at the types of birds in each habitat we see that some species show distinct preferences for one type or another.

In Singapore the Sanderling, Grey Plover, Malaysian Plover and Kentish Plover are confined almost exclusively to sandy shores. On the other hand Black-tailed Godwit, Wood Sandpiper and Curlew Sandpiper seem confined to muddy shores. Others such as Redshank, Greenshank, Rufous-necked Stint, Long-toed Stint, Little Ringed Plover and Pacific Golden Plover can be found on both types of shore but reach much greater concentrations on muddy shores.

An interesting feature related to this, which we can see in Singapore, occurs on the reclaimed land such as that along East Coast Park and around the Changi peninsula. These beaches hold fewer birds than sandy coasts formed by natural wave action. The sand used for the reclamation here is exceptionally coarse in nature and the exposure which these new shorelines receive means that the sand is continually stirred up by wave action. There is less organic matter on this sand than on natural beaches and therefore fewer invertebrate organisms. The only shorebirds which can be seen feeding on these areas are the small plovers (Malaysian, Little Ringed, sometimes Mongolian) and the Sanderling. These birds all feed by picking small animals off the surface of the sand rather than probing into it with their beak. The probing shorebirds are only seen feeding at the mouths of the rivers and drains where a miniature estuary provides a little shelter, where mud can be deposited and therefore where there are a few more invertebrates to be eaten.

Most bird species are strongly affected by the diurnal cycle of light and dark. The majority are only active during daylight hours whilst a few, such as owls and nightjars, are especially equipped to obtain their food at night. But the shorebirds are subject to different environmental influences. Since they are feeding on the shoreline, and often on exposed mudflats, they are forced to respond to the movements of the sea which twice a day causes the tides to wash over their feeding grounds, denying them access to their food. So these shorebirds will feed at night if that is when the low tide occurs and conversely will sleep during the daytime if the high tide has pushed them off their feeding grounds.

At low tide the birds can be seen spread out over a wide expanse of mud. As the tide begins to advance they continue to feed but slowly work their way up the shoreline, keeping a little ahead of the waves and getting more and more bunched together. Becoming more and more compressed near to the top of the shoreline, they finally take off in large flocks to find a safe place to roost until the tide recedes again.

Often these high tide roosting

sites will take the form of a large sand spit extending into the sea, or perhaps a sea wall or even an old jetty. On the newer reclaimed land, which has not been planted yet, they will flock together in the middle of a large open space. Wherever it is, you can be assured that the birds will have a good view of the surrounding area so that a potential predator can be spotted long before getting close.

Many of the shorebirds we see in Singapore are what we term passage migrants, that is they are just staying for a few days to feed up before passing further on their journey. These birds are under pressure to feed as quickly as possible in order to build up the necessary fat reserves which are their fuel supplies for further migratory flight. Thus many of them will seek out alternative places which may provide them with food during the high tide period. This may take the form of a rather unpromising puddle in the middle of a football field, but more often will be a prawn pond.

Most of our prawn ponds are now unused and await reclamation but do form very important high tide locations for shorebirds. They are usually in the form of a large water body enclosed by mud embankments (bunds) with an opening to the sea controlled by a sluice. Sometimes, if the sluice is closed, the pond may be almost empty of water during the high tide period, providing a nice muddy expanse over which the birds can continue to feed. Even in the abandoned ponds the tide cannot penetrate the narrow sluice entrance very quickly and

A **White-breasted Waterhen;** *wetlands form an important but much neglected habitat for birdlife* (photo: Morten Strange).

as much as an hour's extra feeding can be obtained by the birds before it fills up. Once full, of course, the pond empties correspondingly slowly, but by then the birds can move back on to the exposed foreshore.

Many countries exploit these movements of birds and tides to provide excellent bird-watching facilities and bird sanctuaries. There are many opportunities for this in Singapore. However, even in the absence of such facilities the astute birder can utilise them to his own advantage. Look for waders on an advancing tide as they are being pushed up the shore towards you, the flocks becoming steadily more compressed. If you can find a high-tide roosting or feeding place get yourself into position before the birds arrive so that your movements will not scare them away. Don't go birding on an open shore right at high tide — it will be empty — nor at low tide as then the birds will usually be too far away or too spread out for you to see well.

One question which visitors from temperate regions often ask is why we have so few sea-birds. The answer is not properly known but probably lies in the nature of the productivity of surface waters. In the tropics there is a big change in temperature usually about ten metres underwater. This is called the thermocline; colder waters sink below it and waters warmed by the sun float on top (warm water is less dense than cold). Nutrients in the water tend to get locked up in the colder waters at the bottom and so this is where most of the fish are — too deep to be reached by sea-birds. Exceptions occur around coral reefs and steep sea-cliffs where there may be some upwellings, and this is where we find tropical sea-birds. In temperate regions the thermocline breaks down during the cold winter and nutrients are released to the surface waters. So in the spring time there is a massive bloom of productivity at the surface as the waters warm up, providing plenty of food for sea-birds over a very wide area.

This is only a hypothesis; it may equally prove that the tropics lack the type of nesting sites many sea-birds require. This is a good illustration of the research still needed to be done on tropical birds.

Mangroves

In the tropical belt, where the coastal substrate is sufficiently stable, an assemblage of plants collectively known as mangroves are able to grow in the shallower waters. These plants are highly specialised: they can resist the effects of salt water, tolerate very bright sunlight and high temperatures, and can grow in very soft mud which is lacking in oxygen. Once established their root systems have a stabilising effect on the mud and they tend to progress slowly seawards, nature's own reclamation system! In this way vast forests can be built up. However these mangrove formations tend to have rather few species of plants in them, perhaps because of the difficulties of adapting to this type of environment.

Because there is a low plant diversity mangrove forests tend to be less complex in structure than lowland rainforests. The tidal movements mean there is almost no undergrowth and mangrove trees never attain the vast stature of rainforest trees. Thus, although the birds of mangrove are characteristic of these areas, very few are confined to mangrove and most are found in other habitats. It is as though they are less specialised in their habits and can therefore adapt to other areas.

In Singapore many of the birds we see in parks and gardens originated in mangrove: the Common Iora, Pied Triller, Pied Fantail, Collared Kingfisher, Glossy Starling, Olive-backed Sunbird and Brown-capped Woodpecker all seem to have their origins in mangrove. Even though they have been able to spread into parks and gardens they do not reach the same densities there as in their natural habitat.

We have only three species in Singapore which are confined entirely to mangrove: the Mangrove Pitta, Mangrove Blue Flycatcher and Ruddy Kingfisher. The Mangrove Whistler and Ashy Tailorbird are occasionally seen out of mangrove, but seldom far away from it, and their populations are probably totally dependent upon its continued existence. The Laced Woodpecker seems to be slowly spreading inland from mangrove, but whether it is totally independent of it is hard to say.

Mangroves have been important in the economy of South-east Asia ever since man began exploiting natural resources. One of their most important features went unrecognised for a long time and that is their role as a spawning and nursery area for the larvae of many commercially-exploited marine animals — fish, prawns and shellfish. In this connection it is notable that until the last few years the most active fisheries in Singapore were located along the coasts which had the best stands of mangrove. The other aspect of their economic importance was almost in direct competition to this, and that is, their exploitation for timber and timber products which resulted in their total destruction in many areas. The wood has been used for construction purposes, fishing stakes and scaffold poles; it has been burned as firewood and to produce charcoal; the bark has been extracted to produce tannins, and a host of other minor items such as medicines, foods, oils, incense wood and even cigarette wrappers have been taken from mangrove. Once the Singapore mangroves had been worked out for these products they were largely cleared to construct fish and prawn culture ponds, the mangrove trees growing back on the fringes of these and in the river mouths.

In modern Singapore even this type of exploitation is now history and the major threat is from reclamation to provide land-hungry Singapore more space in which to live or barrages to form freshwater reservoirs. The remnants of our mangroves are now found spreading a short distance on either side of the Causeway and around the Seletar and Serangoon Estuaries, and even most of these are slated to disappear shortly.

Removal of the last of Singapore's mangrove will undoubtedly have its repercussions on the birdlife of the island. It will result in the loss of the mangrove birds themselves, of course, but it will also affect the life cycles of the invertebrates upon which the shorebirds feed. It is likely that any remaining mudflats will be less rich in marine life than before and therefore able to feed fewer birds.

Coupled with the physical re-

Common Birds of Mangrove and Edges

Little Heron
Spotted Dove
Plaintive Cuckoo
Collared Kingfisher
Laced Woodpecker
Brown-capped Woodpecker
Pacific Swallow
Pied Triller
Common Iora
Yellow-vented Bulbul
Black-naped Oriole
House Crow
Large-billed Crow
Flyeater
Common Tailorbird
Ashy Tailorbird
Rufous-tailed Tailorbird
Yellow-bellied Prinia
Pied Fantail
Mangrove Whistler
Philippine Glossy Starling
Common Myna
White-vented Myna
Brown-throated Sunbird
Olive-backed Sunbird
Scaly-breasted Munia

clamation of the mudflats the future seems very bleak indeed for many of these species. All are birds which migrate many thousands of kilometres in their annual movements and depend upon Singapore as a major refuelling site or winter quarters. Without their vital refuelling stops thousands may die of starvation before reaching their destination.

Freshwater Wetlands

Although not strictly a coastal habitat, the freshwater swamps of Singapore are all located close to the coasts. It is a very new class of habitat which has been created by the damming of several river mouths to provide shallow reservoirs on the landward side.

The best example is found at Kranji reservoir on the western edge of which a rich freshwater swamp has been formed within the last ten years. These swamps attract many herons, bitterns, rails and migrant warblers. Some of the birds can be found on the seaward side of the dams as well. In addition many of the shorebirds which feed on the coastal mudflats use the freshwater swamps as roosting places when they are pushed off the mud at high tide.

At Kranji there are breeding colonies of Purple and Grey Heron, as well as large numbers of Cinnamon Bitterns and Yellow Bitterns. The latter species has only ever been recorded as a migrant this far south, but we are finding more and more of them at Kranji during their breeding season and whilst in the final stages of writing this book it has been recorded breeding in Singapore. I foresee these areas becoming increasingly important to the Singapore avifauna in years to come, providing they are left to develop naturally and remain undisturbed.

Ornithologically then these two areas — coastal and freshwater wetlands — tend to complement each other. I have compiled a list of 152 species which can be readily assigned to these wetland habitats. This makes them the single richest category of bird habitat on the island, containing over 50 percent of the recorded species, 88 of which cannot be found elsewhere in Singapore.

FOREST

The tropical rainforests of South-east Asia are unique. They have been in existence for 130 million years, and in a few places we can see forests which have been unchanged by the hand of man in all that time. This long period of evolution, punctuated by changing sea levels during the ice-ages, and by small fluctuations in temperature and rainfall, has resulted in the formation of a very complex natural system.

One of the most startling features of the forest has been the evolution of an amazing number of different types of plants — nearly 3,000 species of trees in the Malay Peninsula alone. Although the different plant species tend to be clumped according to their particular habitat requirements, in any one place there tends to be an enormous variety. Studies have shown there to be over 200 species of trees in just one hectare (100m × 100m) of primary forest. This means a great diversity of plants in any one area, greater than in any other habitat on earth.

This staggering variety of plants supports an even greater variety of things which live on and in them. All the plant-chewing insects have their own particular preferences for food plants and one plant may support a myriad of different species. This effect is passed on up the food chain to those animals which eat insects and which are eaten in their turn. With each link in the chain the diversity is reduced so that, near the end of the chain, we end up with about 300 species of inland forest birds in the Malay Peninsula. Each of these species is highly specialised, choosing its own particular selection of the foods the forest has to offer. Each species tends to be an expert in catching or handling the prey that it chooses and sticks to that choice.

In this way the diversity of the forest is maintained and a great number of different species can co-exist in one place. Because of this high degree of specialisation when the forests are disturbed by logging, or cleared for agriculture, many forest birds are unable to survive in the strange environment which is left.

A brief history of the Singapore forests was sketched in the first chapter. The constant high levels of clearance and disturbance resulted in the loss of 87 bird species which were originally found in this habitat. Many of the species found in the forest today have recolonised from the pockets of trees which were all that remained at one time.

Those species which are now extinct in Singapore will not recolonise from elsewhere because of the barrier of open water and cleared land which separates us from forested areas in Malaysia and Indonesia. However, the forest is still an important bird habitat in Singapore and 126 species of birds have been recorded

Common Birds of the Forest

Pink-necked Pigeon
Green-winged Pigeon
Grey-rumped Treeswift
Chestnut-bellied Malkoha
Red-crowned Barbet
Banded Woodpecker
Olive-winged Bulbul
Cream-vented Bulbul
Greater Racket-tailed Drongo
Asian Fairy-bluebird
Short-tailed Babbler
Chestnut-winged Babbler
Striped Tit-babbler
Arctic Warbler
Dark-necked Tailorbird
Philippine Glossy Starling
Hill Myna
Purple-throated Sunbird
Crimson Sunbird
Little Spiderhunter
Orange-bellied Flowerpecker
Scarlet-backed Flowerpecker

there in recent years; 68 of these species are unique to that habitat.

The resident community that we see in the Singapore forest today is interesting in that it represents those species with more robust ecological requirements which have allowed them to survive the unstable history of their habitat. Many of them are birds of secondary forest or forest edge elsewhere in the region, both of these sub-habitats being less stable than primary forest itself. For example, our commonest forest bulbul is the Olive-winged; and two of our surviving babblers are the Striped-tit and Chestnut-winged; the only malkoha to have survived is the Chestnut-bellied. All these are usually restricted to the forest edge and secondary areas where primary forest still exists.

Some anomalies do seem to exist though. Why is the Red-crowned Barbet the only one to have survived when we can find the Blue-eared in similar habitats in Malaysia? Why have the Green Broadbill and the Black-and-Red Broadbill disappeared? The Fairy Bluebird is a reasonably common canopy frugivore, yet with one exception the frugivorous pigeons have been decimated. The Little Spiderhunter has hung on tenaciously whereas the Spectacled, which is even found in some gardens in Malaysia, has been lost.

One anomaly we can account for is the absence of the White-rumped Shama which has undoubtedly been trapped out of existence to supply the Singapore bird singing contests. One final interesting point is the virtual absence of diurnal birds of prey in the forest, whilst the nocturnal Brown Hawk Owl and Collared Scops Owl reach high densities.

There also seems to be some evidence of an extension of the normal habitat range amongst some of the species, presumably due to the absence of close relatives. For example, the Crimson and the Purple-throated Sunbirds, Olive-winged Bulbul and Dark-necked Tailorbird can all be found ranging throughout the forest. All these species are normally confined to the forest edge or clearings and their places inside the forest taken by closely related species.

Also in Singapore we can see some open country species which make use of food sources, mainly fruit, in the forest canopy. The Black-naped Oriole, Philippine Glossy Starling, Common Myna and White-vented Myna all occur spasmodically in the forest. However, they are usually confined to the forest canopy and never venture inside the shaded layers of vegetation

So even in a badly depleted forest such as ours there still exist sufficient unexplained questions to keep researchers happy (or otherwise!) for a good many years.

The loss of so many species may make the reader think that birding in Singapore forests is a comparatively uninteresting occupation. It does have its compensations though. The spectacular Racket-tailed Drongo is more common here than in any other place I know of, likewise the magnificent Crimson Sunbird. The White-bellied Sea-eagle nests on the edge of the forest near the reservoirs and can be seen fishing there. The edges of these reservoirs are fruitful birding areas where both open country and forest species may be viewed in good light. They seem to be particularly favoured by migrant species during autumn (September/

October), and one can expect to see a great variety of birds in these places at this time.

So, although the Singapore forests are not as rich in birdlife as those in other areas, there is still a good variety of things to be seen which are only found in this habitat. It is also instructive to see how the birds have responded to the changes brought about and this helps our understanding of the functioning of the forest system. Finally the forest is still the ultimate challenge to observer skills in detection and identification.

Whilst we are discussing the forest we should briefly mention the reservoirs which are located there. Many people are mystified as to why these are not teeming with waterfowl. But then the whole Malay Peninsula is rather poor in this respect. The reason seems to be that in terms of bird evolution Singapore has never had large stretches of non-riverine open water until very recently.

With a very few exceptions stretches of open freshwater are man-made reservoirs or lakes, most only a little over 100 years old. Because of this very few species of ducks ever migrated in this direction because there was no suitable habitat for them to utilise. This is in contrast with somewhere like India with its many natural swamps and lakes which attract large populations of waterfowl. So although we now have some lakes they are really too new for the birds to have learned to use them in the winter.

OPEN COUNTRY

Those parts of the island not covered in the preceding sections

Common Birds of Parks and Gardens

Pink-necked Pigeon
Spotted-necked Dove
Edible-nest Swiftlet
Black-nest Swiflet
House Swift
Palm Swift
Grey-rumped Treeswift
White-throated Kingfisher
Collard Kingfisher
Blue-throated Bee-eater
Brown-capped Woodpecker
Pied Triller
Common Iora
Yellow-vented Bulbul
Black-naped Oriole
Hwamei
Common Tailorbird
Asian Brown Flycatcher
Flyeater
Arctic Warbler
Richard's Pipit
Brown Shrike
Philippine Glossy Starling
Common Myna

White-vented Myna
Brown-throated Sunbird
Olive-backed Sunbird
Scarlet-backed Flowerpecker
Javan Munia
Scaly-breasted Munia
Eurasian Tree Sparrow

can be conveniently lumped under the general heading "open country". In Singapore this comprises parks, gardens, agricultural areas, old rubber and coconut estates and "wastelands". Although most of these may seem very different from each other to the observer, the birds found there are similar. The very specialised nature of birds in rainforest means that few of them are able to adapt to whatever habitat remains once the forest is cleared. So most of the species which are found in open country originate from a variety of other sources.

The only species which seem to have a forest origin are the Collared Scops Owl, Long-tailed Parakeet, Rufous Woodpecker and Flyeater. We are also getting more records of the Brown Hawk Owl away from forests and it is possible that we are witnessing an interesting extension of habitat acceptability by this species.

In contrast to this, a larger number of open country species seem to have originated from mangrove. Such species as Common Iora, Large-billed Crow, Brahminy Kite, Brown-capped Woodpecker, Common Goldenback Woodpecker, Pied Fantail, Collared Kingfisher, Olive-backed Sunbird, Pacific Swallow and Glossy Starling all probably had their natural origins in mangrove.

Natural open country in the form of the beach scrub of the east coast of Malaysia and the floodbanks of the larger rivers have also made their contributions. From the east coast beaches may have come Blue-breasted Quail, Barred Buttonquail, Spotted Dove, Peaceful Dove, Blue-throated Bee-eater, Yellow-vented Bulbul, Richard's Pipit, Magpie Robin and Large-tailed Nightjar. From the

grasses of the river flood banks we probably have got Greater and Lesser Coucal, Yellow-bellied Prinia and perhaps some munias.

Open country has also found a source of birds in the form of naturally invading species or those which have escaped from captivity and formed viable populations. Amongst the natural invaders we have the Common Myna (perhaps assisted by man), Coppersmith Barbet, Black-naped Oriole, Black-shouldered Kite, Common Tailorbird and Zitting Cisticola. The Pegu Sparrow has spread south to Negri Sembilan and may soon reach Singapore.

Species which have been introduced by man have also added important members to our avifauna; in a large part this is due to the brisk trade in wildlife which has passed through Singapore. Among these we have the House Crow, White-vented Myna, (possibly Common Myna), Javan Munia, Red-whiskered Bulbul, Feral Pigeon, Hwamei, Greater Sulphur-crested Cockatoo, Little Corella, Crested Myna and Black-winged Myna. The Java Sparrow is an introduced species which seems less common now than 60 years ago and the Sooty-headed Bulbul is one which has possibly now died out.

Thus our open country avifauna is a mixture of species with a variety of origins. This is entirely because of the relatively recent occurrence of this type of habitat compared to the history and evolution of our birds. It also accounts for the fact that open country habitats in tropical Asia tend to have fewer species of birds in them than those continents, like Africa, which have large tracts of natural open country such as savanna. Here an avifauna has evolved which is adapted to grassland and open woodland and these birds are able to take more readily to the open habitats created by man.

Peter Ward, a Singapore ornithologist of the 1960s, compared the birds found in a West African garden with his in Singapore and found that the African garden had between two and three times as many species. The grasslands of East Africa have as many species of birds living in them as our lowland rainforest, and all are potential invaders of man-made habitats. So a visitor who compares the birds of a Singapore park with those of one in, say, Nairobi will get a totally false impression of our birdlife.

Having said all this about the rather "unnatural" nature of our open country birdlife, I do not wish to deter the reader from birdwatching in these areas. The old agricultural areas can be particularly rewarding to the newcomer to South-east Asian birds. The pattern of open fields separated by dense copses of tall trees and undergrowth seem to be particularly suited to a high density of birds. Around the fields the light is usually bright, enabling things to be seen clearly. Although most of the birds will be very familiar to Singapore birdwatchers there is always the chance of an unusual migrant turning up at the right time of year. Such winter visitors as the Brown Shrike, Ashy Minivet, Black Drongo, Blue-tailed Bee-eater and Chestnut-winged Cuckoo use our open country as a matter of routine.

But it seems that the farming areas also are soon to be cleared, threatening yet other birds.

Common Birds of Farming and Rural Areas

White-breasted Waterhen
Spotted Dove
Peaceful Dove
Grey-rumped Treeswift
Asian Palm-swift
Long-tailed Parakeet
Greater Coucal
Lesser Coucal
Collard Kingfisher
Dollarbird
Rufous Woodpecker
Laced Woodpecker
Common Goldenback
Brown-capped Woodpecker
Barn Swallow
Common Iora
Yellow-vented Bulbul
Flyeater
Common Tailorbird
Rufous-tailed Tailorbird
Yellow-bellied Prinia
Philippine Glossy Starling
Common Myna
White-vented Myna
Brown-throated Sunbird
Olive-backed Sunbird
Scarlet-backed Flowerpecker
Javan Munia
Scaly-breasted Munia

27

HOW, WHAT AND WHERE

As I hope that this book will stimulate the interest of beginners I will address the problem of actually finding and identifying birds. Anyone who wishes to partake in the absorbing and increasingly popular pastime of birdwatching should seek others with the same interest. Learning the ropes from someone with experience is far better than trying to learn fieldcraft from a book.

The previous chapter showed that one could expect to find different species of birds according to the habitat visited. With the exception of finding and watching shorebirds, the principles to be followed are the same for any habitat.

WHEN

At night most day-active (diurnal) birds are resting. They are unable to see to feed in the dark and therefore seek a safe place to shelter. In the tropics our night-time is virtually 12 hours. Thus for half the day most birds must sit still and conserve their energy. This means that come the dawn these birds are hungry and must move around searching for

Agriculture is still found in Singapore and the fringes of these fields, invaded by wild plants, are rich in birdlife (photo: Ian Lloyd).

food. Also, in the breeding season they may use this time to re-establish their territorial boundaries or re-affirm their bond with their mate, situations which may have temporarily broken down during darkness. Both these activities involve singing or calling and so we have the dawn chorus.

The big upsurge of feeding and singing activity which occurs at dawn makes it the best time of the day for birdwatching. The noise and movements reveal the presence of the birds and therefore enable the birdwatcher to find them. For the birdwatcher it is cooler and more comfortable.

Bird activity seems to reach a peak about an hour after dawn. After this it declines steadily and the period from 1100h to 1600h becomes rather dull. From about 1600h there is a resurgence of activity which goes on until dark as the birds get in their last feed of the day. However, this evening peak of activity never seems to have the same urgency as the morning period and birdwatching is usually not as good.

The breeding season, starting in February and lasting through until about July, is the best time of year to find the resident species. But in September/October we have an influx of migrants from the north and so this is the best time to visit the coastlines and reservoirs looking for migrants.

HOW

A pair of binoculars is essential. For birdwatchers 8×40 or 10×40 are the preferred sizes. Telescopes are likely to discourage the beginner and are better left for the more experienced birdwatcher. Binoculars should always be kept clean and also properly focussed and aligned.

A birdwatcher's walking pace is painfully slow. Sudden movements will scare away the objects of your attention and, in addition, it is impossible to walk quickly and search the vegetation carefully. Always try to walk with the sun behind you so that the light will be reflected back at you, thus avoiding frustrating silhouettes. You should also try to be elevated: it is much easier on the neck to look down into the crown of a tree than up at it. This will also avoid the difficulties of trying to discern plumage colours against a light sky.

Although many birdwatchers prefer to dress in browns and greens, the actual colours you wear seem irrelevant. Birds will see you from a long way off, whether you are dressed all in white or all in brown. Remember that they are used to looking for carefully camouflaged predators which can hide themselves far better than we ever can. What is more important is that your behaviour should not alarm the bird.

If you want to get close to a bird do not approach it directly but walk at an oblique angle as though you had not seen it: if the bird suspects that it is the object of your attention it will tend to become more alarmed.

Cars can make very useful mobile hides and you can often get much nearer to a bird in a car than you could on foot. But do not try to look through windows without winding them down: the dirt and distortion caused by the glass will be magnified by your binoculars and will be a handicap.

Often we can get frustratingly close to a bird which stubbornly refuses to show itself. Under these circumstances the bird's curiosity can sometimes be aroused by kissing the back of one's hand to make a squeaking sound, or by pursing the lips and making a "shushing" noise — a pastime affectionately known as "pishing". These noises are crude approximations of the noises by young birds or those in distress and are often investigated by a bird which would otherwise be hidden.

WHAT IS IT?

Having located a bird the next challenge is to try and identify it. The big temptation is to immediately try and match the bird in front of you with a name in the book. The usual result of this is lots of fumbling during which the bird flies away and the book ends up in the mud! The first thing you should try to do is to take in as many details of the behaviour and appearance of the bird as possible. Most of these will be difficult to remember until you have built up some experience.

A notebook and pencil are essential to note down all the characteristics. Start with a crude sketch of the bird's outline and then mark in the relevant features of its colouration. Note also the beak and tail shape and length of legs and neck. Writing down these things helps to focus the attention and allows the mind to

HEADS AND BEAKS

The shape of the head and beak are important identification features and also offer clues to the type of food or feeding method of the bird.

Seed-eaters such as the finches and munias have strong deep bills for crushing seeds (1). Shrikes catch and crush large insects, the beak is strong with a hook on the end to stop the prey escaping (2), their head and eyes also appear quite large. Swallows and swifts catch insects on the wing, the beak is weak and wide (3) and acts as a scoop in the air. Many insectivorous species have undistinguished beaks but inevitably with a small hook at the end (4), this includes babblers, bulbuls, warblers, ioras etc. Flycatchers take most of their prey in the air and their beaks are weak and wide rather like swifts and swallows (5). Many insectivorous birds have rictal bristles at the base of the beak to direct the prey into the mouth (2, 4, 5). The upper and lower mandible of a woodpecker are pointed so that the closed beak forms a chisel shape (6). A kingfisher's beak is also pointed (9) but the lower mandible is often rather scoop-shaped for holding prey. Another pointed beak is found in the herons and egrets (8) which use it for stabbing, the eyes are set well forward so that binocular vision may be employed to judge the distance to prey items. The beaks of waders which probe in the mud may be straight as in the snipe (10), may curve down, or even up as in the Terek Sandpiper (7). Some, like the snipe, are slightly swollen at the tip as they contain sense organs to help probe for the food. In most waders the eyes are set at the side of the head to allow almost 360° vision as a guard against predators. Plovers are waders which probe less deeply or even pick off the surface of the mud, their beaks are quite short (11). Birds of prey have strong hooked beaks for tearing and cutting flesh (12), some have small notches which are used when crushing bones. A very slender decurved bill (13) belongs to a sunbird or spiderhunter, it is designed for probing inside flowers to extract nectar. Bee-eaters also have a decurved bill but heavier than a sunbird's.

move on to other relevant points. If you really feel your drawing skills are not satisfactory then make some copies of the bird shown in the topographical drawing (page 48) and carry these with you as a template upon which notes and alterations can be made.

Size is an important feature so try to match it to another known species which may be close by, or compare it with the flower, leaf or branch upon which it is standing so that a good estimate of size can be made. Make notes also of its behaviour, is it feeding on anything, does it keep repeating a particular behaviour sequence?

Songs and calls are of immense value for identification of a bird. If you can learn to identify the noises which assail your ears you can quickly learn what birds are around you without having to see them. Unfamiliar sounds can alert you to a possible new species which will be worth looking for.

As experience is built up it will be found that each species can be positively identified by a particular combination of characters. In time you will find yourself carrying these facts in your head.

As experience is gained the many pitfalls involved in identification will become clearer. Plumage patterns will sometimes differ between males and females, between adults and juveniles and between birds in breeding and non-breeding ("winter") plumage. Where these commonly lead to confusion we have illustrated the possible combinations in this book. But of course no series of paintings can ever fully capture all the possible variations which can arise. In the tropics, in particular, different light regimes can alter a bird's appearance: a bird in bright sunlight can look rather washed out on the back, while the belly will be in shade. When they are moving around in trees or in the undergrowth a bird may be in shade so dense that no colours are discernable at all.

Some birds have irridescent feathers which make them change colour according to the direction of the light. The classic example of this must be the sunbirds. It can also occur with plumages which have a high gloss like the Philippine Glossy Starling. Often the irridescent colours complement each other and change from one end of the spectrum to the other.

Dirt or pollutants can change the plumage colours of a bird. Shorebirds will often get muddy, especially the beak and legs, and kingfishers may appear shabby through diving into dirty water.

Some birds will only show certain colours when they are active: the white patches on the wings of the White-throated and Black-capped Kingfishers can only be seen in flight; the Common Tailorbird shows dark streaks on the side of the neck when calling which leads to confusion with the Dark-necked Tailorbird; the white rump of the Curlew Sandpiper is hidden at rest and the same is true of the white trailing edge on the wing of Terek Sandpipers and Redshanks.

This long, and by no means exclusive, list of complications is not intended to deter the observer but rather to draw attention to the many circumstances under which a bird's appearance can change. My advice to the beginner (and the more experienced birdwatcher too) is always keep an open mind and never make a snap decision with a difficult identification until you have as many facts to hand as possible.

TAILS

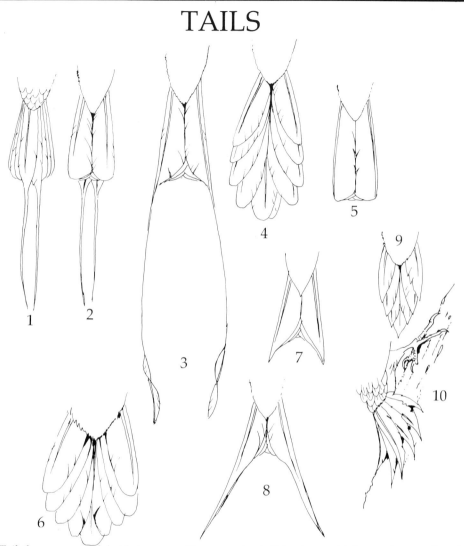

Tail shapes are useful aids to recognition and worthwhile noting carefully in any species which cannot immediately be identified.

In some birds the tail is simply square (5) such as in babblers and bulbuls. A notched tail is formed by the outer tail feathers becoming elongated until a forked tail (7) is formed such as in swallows and swifts. In such as the Barn Swallow, Grey-rumped Treeswift and the Palm Swift the outer tail feathers are so long that a deep fork is formed (8). In the Greater Racket-tailed Drongo (3) it is only the shafts of the outer tail feathers which are elongated and these have a tuft (racket) on the end. In bee-eaters it is the central tail feathers which are elongated and their appearance is different from above (1) and below (2). When the central tail feathers are longer than the outer ones the tail may be rounded (4) as in the Pied Fantail or Chestnut-bellied Malkoha. Wedge-shaped tails are similar (6) and are seen in some birds of prey and the Black-naped Oriole. The woodpecker's is also wedge-shaped (9) but the feathers are stiff to allow the bird to brace itself on a vertical perch.

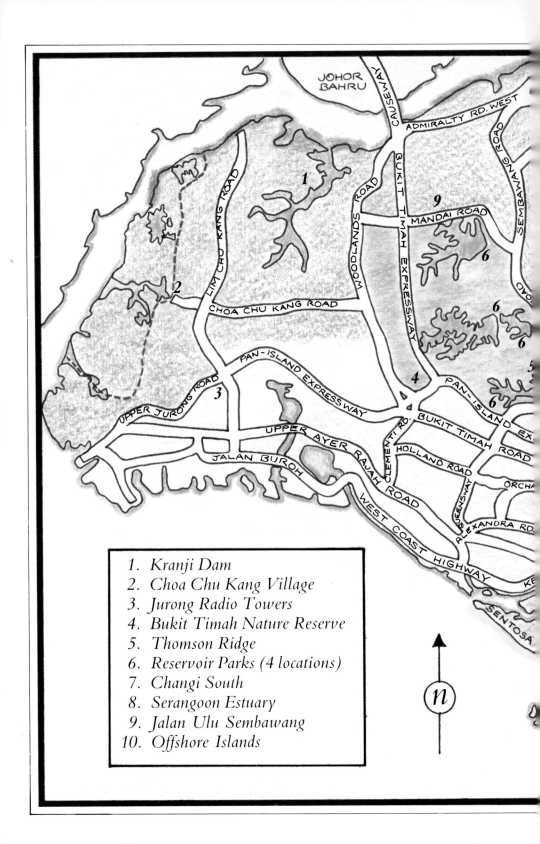

1. Kranji Dam
2. Choa Chu Kang Village
3. Jurong Radio Towers
4. Bukit Timah Nature Reserve
5. Thomson Ridge
6. Reservoir Parks (4 locations)
7. Changi South
8. Serangoon Estuary
9. Jalan Ulu Sembawang
10. Offshore Islands

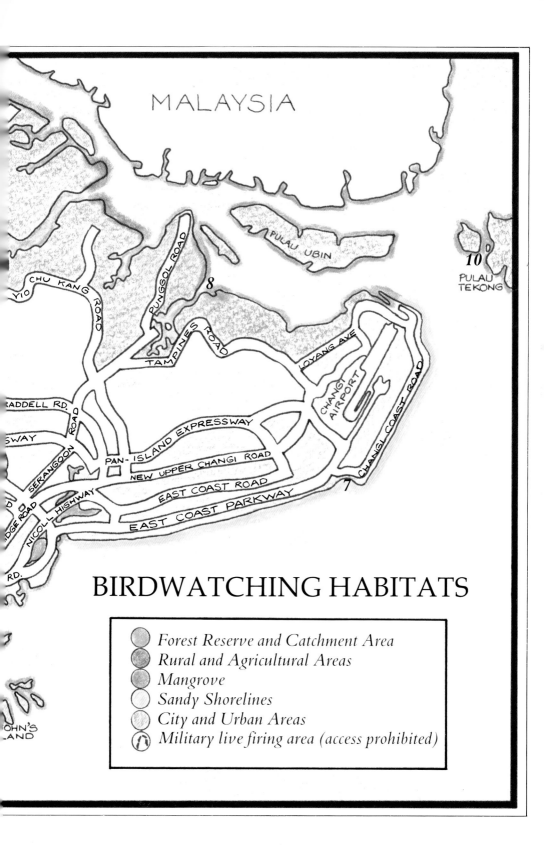

BIRDWATCHING HABITATS

MALAYSIA

PULAU UBIN

PULAU TEKONG

CHU KANG ROAD

YIO

PUNGGOL ROAD

TAMPINES ROAD

LOYANG AVE

CHANGI AIRPORT

CHANGI COAST ROAD

RADDELL RD.

SERANGOON ROAD

PAN-ISLAND EXPRESSWAY

NEW UPPER CHANGI ROAD

EAST COAST ROAD

EAST COAST PARKWAY

NICOLL HIGHWAY

IDGE ROAD

OHN'S AND

- ◯ Forest Reserve and Catchment Area
- ◯ Rural and Agricultural Areas
- ◯ Mangrove
- ◯ Sandy Shorelines
- ◯ City and Urban Areas
- ◯ Military live firing area (access prohibited)

WHERE TO GO

This is probably the first question that any visiting birdwatcher will ask, but even the resident novice birder will also want to know where the better spots are. All the places I will discuss are marked on the island map.

Kranji dam

In the northwest corner of the island the Sungei Kranji has been dammed to form a reservoir. From the dam, good views may be had of terns and sea-eagles over the sea, and herons and osprey over the reservoir. Small areas of mangrove on the seaward side will offer something of interest to those new to this habitat. Mudflats are exposed at low tide and from September to April hold many waders. A car is required to get to the best spot which is accessed by driving over the dam and along Neo Tiew Road to Neo Tiew Lane. From here a track leads through farmland to the Public Utilities Board Kranji Pumping Station (look out for the blue signboard on the main road). Rails, quail and weavers can be found by going carefully through the farmland. At the pumping station walk to the reservoir edge and follow the bund which heads back northwards towards the radio masts. You can find Yellow Bitterns, Cinnamon Bitterns, occasional Schrenks Bittern, Great Reed Warblers, Black-browed Reed Warblers, Zitting Cisticola, Yellow-bellied Prinia, Osprey and Little Tern over the lake, and both Purple and Grey Heron.

Choa Chu Kang village

Continue down Neo Tiew Road until it joins Lim Chu Kang Road and head south to the junction with Choa Chu Kang Road, then head west along the latter to Choa Chu Kang village. A good look around the cemeteries during migration periods is always worth some time. From the village follow Jalan Sungei Poyan south from the centre and take the second track on the right heading towards the sea. Go past the mangrove scrub (look for Ashy Tailorbird and Abbot's Babbler), past the temple and archway (look for Laced Woodpecker) and carry on up to the top of the cemetery hill overlooking the reservoir. With a telescope from here rare migrants have been picked out on the water (Coot and Pintail amongst others) and in the late morning it is a good place to watch for any raptor passage. Do not be tempted into a closer look at the marshes below, as they are in the military live firing area and hence are prohibited.

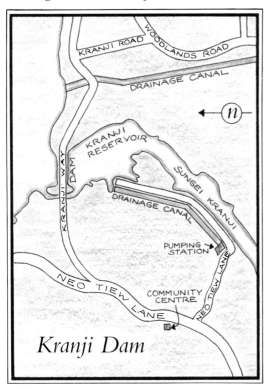

Kranji Dam

Jurong radio towers

Heading south from Choa Chu Kang the next major intersection is with Upper Jurong Road. Head west along this for about half a mile and look for the telecommunication towers on the left. A scan through the fence over the vast area of long grass can often provide the coucals, White-throated Kingfishers, Black-shouldered Kites and Yellow-bellied Prinias. From October to April an added bonus often includes the Black Drongo and the two shrikes.

Bukit Timah Nature Reserve

Birds are difficult to find in the forest, but a visit to the Nature Reserve is a must. Guide books and maps are on sale at the Ranger's Post. Walk up the main trail and then follow Fern Valley Contour path into the Jungle Fall area for an interesting walk. Watch out for Greater Racket-tailed Drongo, Fairy Bluebird, Short-tailed Babbler, Striped Tit-babbler, Banded Woodpecker and maybe a Scarlet Minivet or Blue-winged Leafbird on a good day. Nice views from the top: spinetail swifts in winter.

Even if there are only a few birds to be seen (not unusual) tropical rainforest is one of the most fascinating habitats in the world and there is always something of interest to look at.

Thomson Ridge

Take Upper Thomson Road to the junction with Thomson Ridge on the left, just past the Sin Ming junction. Go along Thomson Ridge, which is a cul-de-sac ending at the forest. A path carries on straight and down about 200m to a wide track running approximately north-south. Walk either way; south takes you to MacRit-

chie Reservoir, north to the Island Country Club. This side of the catchment area contains the best forest away from Bukit Timah Nature Reserve.

Reservoir parks

All the dams in the catchment area have parks, and footpaths into the forest associated with them. The best are at Upper Peirce and Lower Peirce dams, both accessed from Thomson Road (see below). Upper Peirce seems to be particularly good in September/October, when the northern migrants are passing through, perhaps because of the lower forest and generally open aspect of this area. Seletar dam has good areas, but most are now placed out of bounds by the military. MacRitchie dam attracts joggers

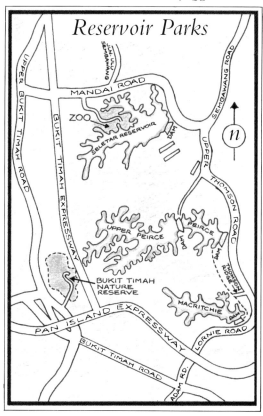

and strollers and is usually too disturbed for birdwatching.

Changi south

A reclaimed sandy coastline but one which supplies some interest during the migration season and the northern winter. Turn off the East Coast Parkway at the sign to Tanah Merah Country Club. About 500m before the club the road passes over a large canal which runs out to sea. Walk to the seaward end of this to find a good selection of sandy shore waders and others, e.g. Mongolian Plover, Little Ringed Plover, Grey Plover and Kentish Plover. Along the seaward beaches to the north look for Malaysian Plover, Sanderling and Ruddy Turnstone.

Serangoon estuary

This is the single richest bird site in Singapore, now steadily being destroyed by reclamation. Like many similar sites elsewhere it is an unsavoury position between the rubbish dump and the sewage works, two establishments which never fail to attract birds, no matter what part of the world you are in! To find it follow Upper Serangoon Road on to Tampines Road (bus 80, 81, 323), and along this until you are travelling parallel to the Paya Lebar Airport runway. Just before the end of the runway, on the left, is Lorong Halus and the entrance to the Ministry of the Environment rubbish dump. At the end of Lorong Halus is the Serangoon sewage works and just before this a new road on the left heading seawards over newly-reclaimed land. This road will take you to the estuary and the remains of several prawn ponds.

Reclamation works are dramatically changing the face of this area so some loose interpretation of my directions may be required in the future. But from October until April the estuary is home for up to 20,000 shorebirds of mixed species. At low tide they feed in the estuary and at high tide pack into the ponds in spectacular numbers. Pacific Golden Plover and Redshank predominate, but literally any of the shorebirds in the Checklist could be found here, and probably one or two we have yet to document. All our egrets and herons occur here, including the very rare Chinese Egret. There are snipe and quail in the field around the sewage works.

At the time of writing we are all watching the future of the area with great concern. If the reclamation works totally destroy the bird habitats of the area, as they seem likely to do, there will undoubtedly be several more species which

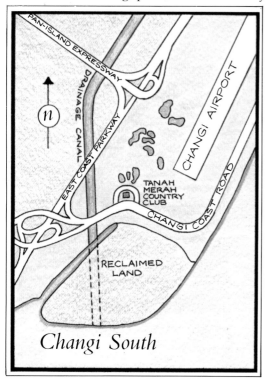

Changi South

we will have to delete from the Checklist as this is the only Singapore location for them.

Jalan Ulu Sembawang

To the north of Mandai Road Jalan Ulu Sembawang winds its way over low hills and through farmland in what is one of the last of Singapore's rural areas. It provides an interesting walk to the visitor which will reveal just about all of our open country species. Not far from here is the Zoo, worth a visit to see some Asian mammals. It is well landscaped, and always with a few birds to offer. The entrance road should provide good forest edge birdwatching.

Offshore islands

Some of the offshore islands are worth visiting and are easily accessed. To the south is St. John's, a small island and therefore one with several species — which are otherwise found on the mainland — missing. For reasons which are not exactly clear there is a high density of feral species here, notables being Black-winged and Chinese-crested Mynas, and also several parrots. Coppersmith Barbets are easily found here as well as Magpie Robins.

Ferries from the World Trade Centre run once a day during the week but almost every hour on Sundays and public holidays — check the times and don't get stranded!

To the north we have Pulau Ubin and Pulau Tekong. The latter may soon be closed by the military but is our only site for Ruddy Kingfisher, Mangrove Blue Flycatcher and Mangrove Pitta. Pulau Ubin has historically always been fairly rich, perhaps because of the close proximity to Malaysia. Heavy quarrying activities have un-

fortunately ensured the extinction of all the forest species; however it is still the only place to guarantee seeing Straw-headed Bulbul. Magpie Robins are not uncommon and there may be other things still lurking there waiting to be found. Ferries to both Tekong and Ubin go from Changi Point. They leave whenever they are full.

Clearly this list of a few sites does not cover all the birding spots in Singapore. It does include the best and also a few personal favourites. Everyone eventually works up their own "patch" which they consider to be the best, and the more of these that can be identified the better.

I am sure that even in crowded Singapore there still remain one or two good bird sites which have not yet come to the attention of birdwatchers.

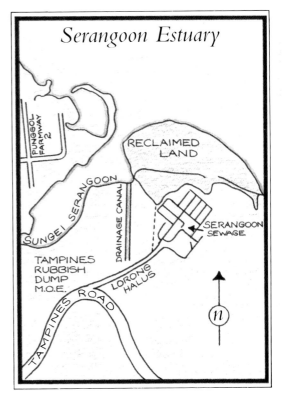

THROUGH THE SEASONS

The Checklist at the back of this book contains 295 species of birds which have been recorded in Singapore within the last 10 years. Records older than this have been omitted because the rapid change in Singapore's development has meant that some of these species have been lost.

Not all of the 295 species are present throughout the year. Only 118 are resident birds which means that they are present all year round and breed here. During the annual migrations into, or through, South-east Asia a further 141 species can be seen. Only 94 of these occur reliably in reasonable numbers and approximately 47 are rare visitors: 24 species turn up unpredictably as vagrants and there are 12 non-native species which appear to have begun as escapes or releases from captivity.

MIGRANTS

Migrant species begin to arrive in Singapore as early as June or July but the bulk arrive in the period beginning September through to November, with a few appearing as late as December.

The **White-bellied Sea-eagle,** *like most birds of prey, often breeds earlier than other species, from December to March* (photo: Kang Nee).

The reverse occurs from March to late May with the majority of the birds making a return migration to their breeding grounds. Almost all of our migrants breed in an area east of the 90th meridian. Birds west of that line migrate mostly to Africa.

Not all of our migrant species travel the same distance or breed in the same areas. Whilst most of them breed in the north temperate or arctic zone, others only come from sub-tropical or even tropical zones north of here.

Some species which we classify as resident are represented further north by migratory populations so that during the northern winter we can have two groups of these birds, the resident Singapore population and a group of migrant visitors. This is the case with the Little Heron, Brown Hawk Owl and White-breasted Waterhen. It may be that the migrant form of the Drongo Cuckoo also reaches Singapore.

As a general rule those birds from the furthest north tend to migrate further south and so these species pass through Singapore twice a year, stopping here only for brief periods on their journey. For example, in 1984 the "Interwader" team colour-marked 400 migrant

Curlew Sandpipers and one of these was later seen in North Western Australia. Those birds from lower latitudes tend to travel less far and some may spend all their "winter" in Singapore.

In the Checklist at the back of this book you will see that these two groups are distinguished from each other as "migrants" or "winter visitors". I am sure the reader is aware that establishing the distinction between these two groups requires systematic observations and in many cases our information is poor: it is almost certain that some of the status indications in the Checklist will require revision at a later date.

There is only one species which breeds in Singapore and then moves south. The Blue-throated Bee-eater, an open country bird, breeds from late February/early March until about September. Outside these months small numbers can be seen around the edge of the catchment area forests, and these are assumed to be winter visitors from further north. This shift from open country to forest is matched by the arrival of the Blue-tailed Bee-eater from areas to the north which seems to take over in the open country in the "winter".

Being almost on the equator we could perhaps expect to see an influx of birds from the south during the southern winter from April to October. In practice this rarely happens as there is little land in the higher latitudes of the southern hemisphere and most migration occurs within the southern continents. However, Wilson's Storm Petrel is a southern bird which has been recorded in the Straits of Malacca. There are also records of Horsfields' Bronze Cuckoo and probably southern hemisphere Ospreys.

Most birds on migration have to carefully apportion their time between flying and feeding. Many birds fly at night, navigating by the stars, and feed during the day. Birds such as swallows, swifts and bee-eaters, which feed on the wing, migrate during the day.

Birds of prey are also day-time migrants, but for a different reason. These very large birds are energetically less efficient at flying than small birds and in order to reduce the energy required for long distance flights raptors use thermals to gain height. They then go into a long, shallow glide in the direction of travel before finding another thermal and repeating the process. In this way they avoid energy-demanding flapping flight as much as possible.

Smaller birds with less wing area are unable to fly like this and so must flap their wings in the normal manner. In doing so they use up energy which is carried in the body in the form of fat reserves. Some small birds can double their weight in a few days by laying down these fat deposits. They may then take off and fly for up to five days and nights before landing to feed again. As the fat is converted to energy, water is produced so they don't need to drink.

Migrating birds use a series of different cues to navigate. They can determine direction using the sun, moon or stars. Proteins containing iron molecules have been found in the brain of some birds which are thought to help them to detect the earth's magnetic field. They also learn to recognise landmarks leading to their home range and recent work in Italy suggests they may even use their sense of smell. Many of these navigation systems also require that the birds have a good sense of time, which must be provided by internal rhythms as yet unidentified.

Since most of the navigational systems require vision, many birds become disoriented in bad weather and will drop onto the nearest land. Night flying migrants are often attracted to bright lights under these circumstances and in Singapore we have had both Hooded and Blue-winged Pitta fly into buildings in this way. This is also the cause of birds being attracted by lighthouses.

Because of the occasional necessity to make "emergency landings", migration routes traditionally avoid long sea or ocean crossings as much as possible. In South-east Asia there are two major routes for birds heading south. One takes them from China over Taiwan and then on an island hop down through the Philippines into Borneo and the Lesser Sundas. Another route takes them across Indo-China through Thailand and down through the length of the Malay Peninsula from where a short crossing to Sumatra can be made. A less frequented route involves a crossing of the South China Sea from the coast of Vietnam to Malaysia.

The Malay peninsula forms a land extension from central .Asia and so forms a natural flyway for birds on migration. Since Singapore is situated at the point of the peninsula, the migrating birds tend to concentrate here before spreading out over the Indonesian islands or even heading to Australia.

Birds seem to pass through Peninsular Malaysia along three routes. A major route, used by many of the birds of prey, follows the western coastal plain. Birds using this cross to Sumatra from Cape Rachado near Port Dickson. A route of lesser importance for birds of prey follows the east coast. Netting studies at Fraser's Hill have shown that many birds also follow the central Main Range of hills and mountains. It is possible that these two latter streams converge on Singapore because

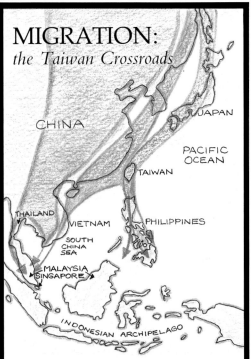

MIGRATION:
the Taiwan Crossroads

The major routes and complexities of migration in South-east Asia are aptly demonstrated by the migration of the Barn Swallow (*Hirundo rustica*). Studies of ringed birds have shown that birds from the continental part of east Asia pass through Thailand and into Malaysia and Singapore. Those from Japan pass through Taiwan and into the Philippines. Those from the eastern seaboard will either pass through Taiwan and south into the Philippines or keep heading west and into Thailand and Malaysia. So Taiwan sees two streams of birds, one going south and the other heading south-west.

we seem to receive a large concentration of migrants from September through to November.

Interestingly, we also seem to see rather more very rare species and vagrants in Singapore than have been observed in any single place in Malaysia. These two facts are consistent with the theory that Singapore is on a migration line.

Visible migration can be seen around the coastlines in the form of the arrival and departure of shorebirds. Birds of prey can be seen soaring in thermals after about 10.00h or 11.00h when the daily temperature has begun to rise. Good places to watch this are on top of the hill overlooking Poyan Reservoir, near Choa Chu Kang village, and Mount Faber nearer the city. From this latter site birds can be seen passing south into the Riau Archipelago.

VAGRANTS

Some of the birds on the Singapore list appear spasmodically, usually in the "autumn" or "winter" period. These are termed vagrants as their movements do not have the consistency of timing or direction which the definition of migration requires. The classic group of birds which come under this category are the frugivorous pigeons, such as the Thick-billed and Little Green Pigeons, and the Jambu Fruit Dove. Whether these birds are dispersing from high population areas or are in search of new food supplies is unknown.

We also record the occasional appearance of forest species which are not known to be resident in Singapore. Why these birds move away from their natal forests is a mystery waiting to be solved.

REFUELLING:
Singapore stopover

The Curlew Sandpiper (*Calidris ferruginea*) is a small (about 60g) shorebird which breeds on the permafrost of the high-arctic tundra. In August/ September 1983 the "Interwader" study team netted 242 of them in Singapore and marked them with a blue dye. After release all the coloured birds disappeared and on November 9, 1983 one was sighted at Port Hedland in northwest Australia. This provided the first direct evidence that some of the shorebirds which winter in Australia use the mudflats of our region as refuelling points. This particular bird flew a minimum of 12,400 km, but we know that they can travel even further than this as they are seen each winter on the southern shores of Australia.

RESIDENTS

Our resident species lead a fairly sedentary existence compared to migrants, but their year is not without significant events. The two major periods are breeding and moulting and these are the times when peak demands are placed upon the metabolism of the individual. Presumably to spread the demand placed upon the bird these two events are usually separated in time.

The breeding season is the most stressful period for resident birds with courting, nest-building, parenting of eggs and nestlings all placing a heavy demand on time and energy. There are hundreds of fascinating reproductive adaptions which are aimed at achieving the most efficient use of resources and maximising success in the form of independent offspring. Courtship displays and rituals may be long and complicated to ensure that both partners are fully committed to assist the other in the reproductive attempt. Many species develop a special nuptial plumage to maximise display or to minimise their conspicuousness to predators.

Eggs are particularly vulnerable to predators and the vagaries of the weather. Nests therefore have to provide an insulated environment whilst remaining as inconspicuous as possible. In tropical areas there is a great variety of animals which could prey upon eggs. To combat this, nests in the tropics tend to be either well-concealed or inaccessible. The classic example of the latter is the nest of the Baya Weaver which, in Singapore, hangs most often from palm fronds. The Palm Swift also has a particularly inaccessible nest.

The sunbirds sometimes build their nests in accessible places but the Olive-backed Sunbird decorates the outside with a variety of items to disguise its presence. Sometimes these birds nest in association with biting ants which will attack any visitors but appear to leave the birds alone. The Rufous Woodpecker goes one step further by burrowing its nest hole into the nest of arboreal ants. The Large-tailed Nightjar lays its two pink eggs in a bare scrape on the ground amongst the leaf litter, relying on its own camouflage to hide them by sitting on the nest during the daytime. At night, when the nightjar is feeding, the eggs are less visible and do not have a bulky nest to attract attention.

For all these reasons, and a few more besides, I have found that locating nests in the tropics is much harder than in temperate regions. It is perhaps significant that there is only one publication on the nesting habits of Singapore birds. This is the work of J. S. Spittle and associates and was based on their detailed observations made while they were inmates of the Changi P.O.W. Camp from 1942 to 1944.

When the eggs hatch, the parent birds have to supply all the food which the nestlings require. For most species this means actively collecting food items and delivering them to the young. At this time the amount of food the parents must gather each day is double or even triple that which they normally gather simply to feed themselves. For this reason it is important that breeding is timed to coincide with the time of year when food is most abundant. In particular, food must be readily available at the critical time when the juvenile birds are becoming independent from their parents and learning to forage for themselves. Since the parents must begin laying the eggs some weeks before this time they must predict the future food supply.

In temperate regions the period when the birds must begin laying corresponds to that time of year when the daylight hours are increasing (springtime). The extra hours of daylight stimulate the hormone system of the birds and this initiates breeding. In the tropics, day-length changes are too small to be effective in this way and so birds must take their cues from elsewhere. In those parts of the tropics with a distinct wet or dry season it is usually the onset of the rains which leads to a flush of food some weeks later, and so this provides a suitable trigger.

In the humid tropics, differences between wet and dry seasons are less marked and scientists do not yet know exactly what the breeding stimulus is in this situation. It is very likely that it is the food supply itself. Increased food intake brought about by a flush of food, or some other improvement in feeding conditions, may result in an improvement in body condition which then stimulates the reproductive process. Thus it is still the environment, mediated by the body condition of the bird, which provides the breeding trigger.

Using Spittle's data, records held at the University of Malaya Nest Record Card Scheme, and additional observations of my own, I have constructed a graph showing the number of species breeding in each month of the year in Singapore. The breeding season appears to commence in December, rising to a peak in April and declining steadily until September. Only October and November have no records.

Not all the species are breeding thoughout these months, although some certainly do show a very protracted breeding season. We have breeding records of Yellow-vented Bulbul from December through to August; for Common Tailorbird from January to September and for Pied Fantail from January to July. In general birds of prey seem to start a little earlier than most species and are amongst the December/January layers. Even in those species, which show a protracted season, not all the individuals will be breeding all the time. Most pairs will raise two broods of young and, exceptionally, three.

However, since bird nests in the tropics are highly susceptible to predation, losses of eggs and nestlings are high. For example,

NUMBER OF BIRD SPECIES BREEDING IN EACH MONTH IN SINGAPORE

the Pacific Swallow fails in 72 percent of its breeding attempts and the losses in birds with more accessible nests are probably even higher. When eggs or nestlings are stolen the parents will, after a short delay, begin all over again and this may be repeated four or five times in the season if necessary. So, allowing for several failures, a six-month breeding season may well be necessary to raise two broods. Usually once two successes have been registered breeding will stop, even if the season is not yet at an end.

Most insectivorous birds lay only two to three eggs, about half the number of their temperate counterparts. At one time biologists thought that this was due to the shorter tropical day-length which leaves less time for gathering food for nestlings. But further studies have shown that changes in clutch size do not mirror day-length changes exactly. The final explanation is still not clear but it seems likely that it is due to differences in the absolute amount of food available. In temperate regions the summer boom in food supply allows many young to be fed, while in the tropics the "summer" food level is not so high but is fairly stable throughout the year, due to the absence of "winter".

Once the breeding season is over most birds will immediately enter a period of moulting. Feathers do not grow continuously and so become worn over time. Since they act as an insulation layer, a waterproof covering and, in the wings, allow the bird to fly, they must be maintained in good condition and so regular replacement is essential. Typically all feathers are replaced at least once a year. Since the feathers of a small bird may account for five to 10 percent of its weight a considerable amount of energy is necessary for their replacement.

Each successive generation of feathers grows in the same spot. A new feather is encased in a sheath and as it grows through the skin it pushes the old one out. So, for a few days, a gap may appear. This is often noticeable in the wings and seems particularly obvious in the crows and the Black-naped Oriole. Gaps in the wings must affect flight efficiency and so those species which are particularly dependent upon flight, like the aerial feeders (swifts and swallows), will only moult one feather at a time.

Some birds undergo a minor moult just before the breeding season and at this time the new plumage may contain the brighter feathers used in breeding displays. The most striking example of this in Singapore occurs in the White-winged Tern which changes colour almost completely. At this time we see the breeding plumages of some of the waders and the handsome plumes of the egrets, while the male Common Tailorbird gets his long tail and the Racket-tailed Drongo its rackets.

Many young birds have rather drab colours and this has survival value, making them less obvious to predators. Some of these drab colours may be lost at the end of the breeding season in which the birds hatched, but they usually undergo only a partial moult at this time as they are still learning to fend for themselves and their "spare" energy may be limited. The full adult plumage is not usually attained until the beginning of the following breeding season when another partial moult is carried out.

TOPOGRAPHY OF A BIRD

It is not necessary to try and learn all the details of the different parts of a bird. But this guide will be useful in understanding some of the terms used in the text and will also allow some of the more descriptive English names to be meaningful.

1. Lower mandible.
2. Upper mandible.
3. Forehead.
4. Lores.
5. Crown.
6. Eyering.
7. Ear coverts.
8. Nape.
9. Back.
10. Tertiaries.
11. Secondaries.
12. Primaries.
13. Rump.
14. Upper tail coverts.
15. Tail.
16. Tarsus.
17. Claw.
18. Toe.
19. Thigh.
20. Flank.
21. Belly.
22. Primary coverts.
23. Greater wing coverts.
24. Median wing coverts.
25. Lesser wing coverts.
26. Breast.
27. Throat.
28. Chin.
29. Leading edge of wing.
30. Wing tip.
31. Trailing edge of wing.
32. Axillaries.
33. Wing lining.
34. Under tail coverts.

COMMON BIRDS OF SINGAPORE

A systematic account
of their habits, status,
and distribution.

1. GREY HERON *(Ardea cinerea)* (40"/102cm)

This is the largest bird in Singapore and although it may be confused with the next species when in flight, the plumage is very distinctive. In flight it has a ponderous wingbeat and a rather hunched posture whilst at rest. The sexes are similar except that the plumes of the female are shorter. It seems to have done very well in Singapore over recent years: only two previous breeding localities were known in this part of the world, one in Perak and one in Selangor. Singapore now has the third. As elsewhere in the region it seems to prefer coastal mudflats and river mouths for its fishing. It can be seen on almost any day by scanning the mudflats along the coastline between Changi and Kranji. The latter place affords the best views, and an observer standing on the dam can see them flying overhead between the freshwater marshes and the sea. Birds will often also stand on the fish culture cages which float in the Kranji reservoir, to loaf, preen or sunbathe. Heronries elsewhere have suffered heavily, and even been destroyed by indiscriminate pillaging of the nest for eggs and nestlings. If this can be prevented in Singapore, and the breeding grounds preserved, we may well have a large population of these birds in the future.

2. PURPLE HERON *(Ardea purpurea)* (38"/97cm)

Elsewhere in the region this bird frequents inland marshes and swamps, but in Singapore it is predominantly a bird of the coasts. It can be seen in similar habitats to the Grey Heron, catching fish, frogs, reptiles, insects and smaller marsh birds with the same stealthy movements and stabbing action. It tends to be rather retiring by day, feeding chiefly in the early morning and late evening. In flight it can be confused with the Grey Heron — both large birds with dark primaries. The more slender neck of the Purple Heron is folded back in flight, giving it a pouched or keeled appearance. At close range the purple colouration is unmistakable whilst in silhouette the neck appears more slender and snake-like than that of the Grey. Again, this bird has recently been found to be breeding in Singapore when the only previous known sites were in Kedah and Perak. It migrates from the north and birds ringed in the U.S.S.R. have turned up in the peninsula. Regular counts are required to see whether the Singapore population is swelled by immigrants from the north.

3. LITTLE HERON *(Butorides striatus)* (18"/46cm)

This is probably one of the most familiar birds of our shoreline and can be seen hunting all around the coast, with the exception of the very sandy areas formed by reclamation. It may also occasionally be seen in the central catchment area on the edges of the reservoirs. We have two separate populations — one resident all year and the other a winter visitor from the north. The latter includes members of a slightly larger sub-species, a difference not detectable in the field. This small heron feeds by creeping along the water's edge or over open mudflats in a hunched crouch, often flicking its crest up and down. It usually prefers to be close to vegetation, but at low tide can be seen dotted over a wide expanse of mud. Upon spotting prey it will lunge forwards, sometimes diving almost under the surface of the water. It will crouch on the spars of jetties or fish cages and stab at fish in the water. It feeds on crustaceans, fish, insects and amphibians. It is a very cautious bird and will never let one approach too near without taking off in a very low flight, with droopy wings, sometimes uttering the "kwenk" alarm call. It has been recorded as nesting in mangroves in loose colonies of up to ten pairs, but the nests are not easily seen in Singapore, despite the large number of these birds that seem to be around.

4. LITTLE EGRET *(Egretta garzetta)* (24"/61cm)

This is the smallest of the white egrets which feeds on the foreshore (but refer to Cattle Egret) and the most easily identified. All year round it has black legs and a black bill with greenish yellow feet. One rarer subspecies, which has been found in this region, has the yellow confined to the soles of the feet. The beak always seems proportionately longer than in other species; like a big black stiletto. In breeding plumage it develops long plumes on the breast and back, the latter hanging down to the end of the tail; and two beautiful long ones on the head hang down the neck, sometimes slightly curled up when blowing in the wind. It feeds in a very enthusiastic manner, often dashing up and down in the shallows, stabbing at prey in a flurry of spray. It invariably feeds in flocks and I have seen up to 40 at a time feeding in the Serangoon estuary. Studies in the Camargue in France have shown that this species catches more food when the flocks are larger, seemingly because they all converge on places where the prey is most dense, in contrast with species with the "sit and wait" type of strategy, like the Great Egret which tend to feed more successfully when well spaced out. An alternative fishing method is to stand in a low crouch with the wings spread either side of the body — perhaps a means of obscuring the glare of the sun, but there is another possiblity. A method of fishing used off the coast of Trengganu and Pahang involve floating fronds of coconut palms in the water and then catching fish which are attracted to the shadow. Perhaps the Little Egret is doing this also by attracting fish into the shade created by its outstretched wings? If this were the case it would be interesting to speculate who learned the method from whom! Slightly less speculative is the knowledge that the Little Egret is a non-breeding visitor to the region from September to May. The breeding plumage has been seen as early as February so there is plenty of time to enjoy their splendour.

5. CHINESE EGRET *(Egretta eulophotes)* (27"/69cm)

This is one of Singapore's "star" birds. At one time it was fairly common but in the last century was heavily persecuted for its elaborate plumes (aigrettes), required to decorate the hats of fashionable ladies. Nowadays it is listed in the I.U.C.N.'s Red Data Book as endangered. It breeds in Korea and China and formerly in Hong Kong. The exact size of the world population is unknown: breeding sites are difficult to reach and when it migrates south to winter it seems to spread out thinly through S.E. Asia, undoubtedly in places with no ornithologists to record its presence. Small numbers have been recorded in Singapore almost every winter since 1973, mostly in the Serangoon estuary where it mixes with other white egrets. This latter habit makes estimating numbers very difficult since in winter plumage it can be mistaken for the white-phase Reef Egret whose colouration is virtually identical. In summer plumage the combination of yellow bill, black legs, yellow toes and short shaggy crest are shared with no other species. Unfortunately, just as the birds which winter in Singapore are attaining their nuptial beauty, numbers begin to decline as they take off for their summer quarters. Thus a certain amount of doubt always exists as to the exact number around. Most reliable estimates are somewhere between six and fifteen.

6. CATTLE EGRET *(Bubulcus ibis)* (20"/51cm)

This bird takes its name from its association with cattle in pastures and padi fields, feeding on the insects which are disturbed by the larger animals. The opportunities for this type of behaviour in modern Singapore are somewhat limited and thus it is found only in a few localities. I have only ever seen it in any numbers on grassland near the mouth of the Serangoon River and in the farming areas around Punggol. There are no breeding records south of Thailand and it would appear to be a winter visitor. At the end of the winter most individuals attain their nuptial plumage before departing for the breeding grounds. Although it can be seen in mangrove areas roosting with other white egrets it rarely feeds with any of these. It is much shorter and stockier than the other egrets, the bill is more blunt and it has a little frill of feathers under the lower mandible which give it a rather jowled appearance. In breeding plumage the buff to orange shaggy feathers on the crown, throat and mantle are distinctive. It usually carries the neck hunched down into the shoulders, but when searching for insects it will stretch it out and walk with a swaying action like a goose.

53

Identifying the Commoner White Egrets

	REEF[1]	GREAT	LITTLE	CHINESE
SIZE	23″/58 cm	35″/89 cm	24″/61 cm	27″/69 cm
LEGS	greenish	black	black with yellow toes	greenish-yellow (w); black with yellow toes (s)
CREST[2]	very short tuft	none	two long plumes	short & shaggy
BEAK	yellow	yellow (w) black (s)	black	black or dark (w) yellow (s)
OTHER	–	kink in neck	long pointed beak	blue facial skin

N.B. 1. Reef Egret — white phase only
2. Crests in summer plumage only

7. GREAT EGRET (*Egretta alba*) (35"/89cm)

Although this bird has been recorded as breeding as far south as Selangor, and there are sight records in Singapore for just about every month of the year, it would appear to be a non-breeding visitor. Commonly seen in the Serangoon estuary in winter, it occurs mostly in the coastal area from Changi to Kranji, often in the company of other white egrets. It is easily distinguished because it is the largest of the egrets and towers over all the others. At a distance the most conspicuous characteristic, apart from the size, is the peculiar kink in the neck about two inches from the head. In winter the bill is yellow and the legs blackish with a green tinge; in summer the bill turns black and the thighs may go yellow, even red, at the height of breeding activity. In breeding plumage the long plumes of the back may extend well beyond the end of the tail. It is very sedate in its behaviour, moving slowly in search of prey, very often with its head bent over to one side. On other occasions it may stand rock still with the head bent forward waiting for prey to come within reach, whereupon it strikes with amazing speed. This is very much in contrast with the mad careering around of the Little Egrets who often feed in its company. The habit of tilting the neck to one side when fishing can be seen in a wide variety of herons, but seems to be especially noticeable in this bird. Studies on the Great Blue Heron in Canada strongly suggest that the reason is to move the reflection of the sun from the area over which the neck can strike so that the bird is not blinded by the image of the sun on the water. This would be especially important in turbid waters which the birds experience around Singapore. The food consists mainly of fish but they will eat molluscs, crustaceans, insects and even small mammals and birds. They are usually seen well spread out over an area as though they have no wish to interfere with each other (see a discussion of feeding tactics under the Little Egret). The flight is very graceful with deep, slow wingbeats.

8. PACIFIC REEF-EGRET (*Egretta sacra*) (23"/58cm)

There are two colour phases or morphs of the Reef Egret: one is pure white whilst the other is slate grey. Mixed piebald versions do occur; I have not seen these in Singapore but certainly both of the normal phases may be seen quite easily. As the name suggests it is a bird of rocky coastlines and is best seen on the southern islands at low tide when the fringing coral reefs are exposed. There both morphs may be seen together, stalking over the rocks, probing in the pools and shallows in search of food. It does occasionally visit mudflats and I have seen it in association with other white egrets in the Serangoon estuary. In these situations, however, it tends to stay on firm ground around the water's edge and avoids the softer mud where the other egrets commonly feed. It breeds in this region and the nest is built in low vegetation, usually on rocky cliff ledges; however this type of habitat only occurs on some of the southern islands.

9 imm.

ad.

9. BLACK-CROWNED NIGHT-HERON *(Nycticorax nycticorax)* (24"/61cm)

The squat appearance and very sleek grey plumage of this bird separates it immediately from its relatives. As the name suggests, this bird is predominantly nocturnal, although a few can always be found feeding during the daytime. At the only known breeding colony in Perak they nest in mangroves and fly inland at dusk to feed in the padi-fields. They do make mass directional movements at night in Singapore, but these seem to be mostly along the coast. After dark they can be detected by their characteristic call — a throaty "wok" or "quack". Numbers in Singapore seem to have increased in recent years: although it was recorded from Punggol as long ago as 1915 it was classified only as a vagrant to our shores.

But now, certainly in the Serangoon estuary, it is a well established member of the community. I have a maximum count of 124 flighting overhead there in the direction of Changi before it got too dark to see. Small numbers have also been seen on an island in Jurong Lake. We have not yet recorded breeding but have seen very young birds which seem unlikely to have travelled all the way from Perak. At this latter colony, breeding begins in August and young birds have been known to disperse as far south as northern Johore. The young are very streaky in appearance — most unlike the adults — and one may be forgiven for thinking, on first acquaintance, that they are a different species.

10. YELLOW BITTERN (*Ixobrychus sinensis*) (15"/38cm)

This is one of the smallest of the bitterns in our region. It is a light brown colour above and almost a creamy white below. In flight the most distinctive feature is the black flight feathers which contrast with the light brown wings and back. Since this bird is very difficult to see other than in flight, identification is usually certain! However one must be quick since the flights are normally brief. It frequents marshy areas and reed beds, always in fresh-water. When stalking in the reeds it is very secretive and usually solitary and will adopt the usual bittern posture of "freezing" when disturbed. In this position the neck is held erect and the beak pointed towards the sky, the streaks on the neck and breast match the vertical stripes of the surrounding grass or reeds so that the bird becomes almost invisible. A bittern's eyes are positioned so that it is then able to watch its potential aggressor using both eyes. Most texts describe this species as less common than the next, but in Singapore this would appear to be reversed, especially at the Kranji reservoir where it occurs in large numbers. This may be because of the large number of birds which make this area their winter quarters. For several years now we have had an increasing number of sightings of this bird during the middle months of the year. Just as this book reached proof stage the discovery of a nest with young has confirmed a growing suspicion that it is breeding in Singapore.

11. CINNAMON BITTERN (*Ixobrychus cinnamomeus*) (15"/38cm)

A little larger than the preceding species, it is distinguished from it by the darker chestnut colouration and the uniform brown wings. It frequents fresh-water marshes and is best found at Kranji reservoir. Again, this species is difficult to see unless it is flushed, whereupon it usually only flies a short distance before dropping down very abruptly into the long grass or reeds. It usually occurs singly, but where you find one there will usually be others nearby. It is assumed to breed in Singapore but there seem to be no recent nest records. The nests are reputedly difficult to find, so much so in fact that a Malay story says that if a man wears one on his head he becomes invisible. In Malaysia there is evidence that a non-breeding population arrives from the north, but we do not know whether these birds reach Singapore.

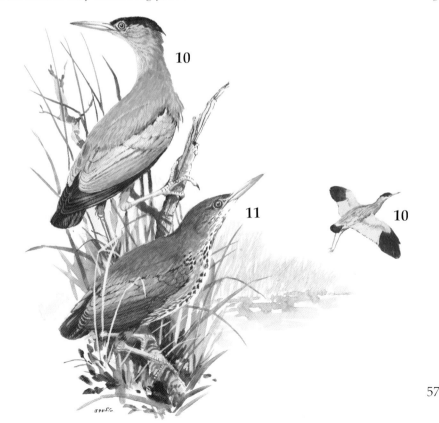

12

12. OSPREY (*Pandion haliaetus*) (22″/56cm)

To the north the Osprey breeds in an unbroken circle across Russia, North America and Europe. To the south it breeds in Australia and eastern Indonesia. Although it can be seen almost year-round in Singapore there is no evidence that it breeds here. It is assumed that birds recorded from October to May are migrants from the north, whilst those during the remainder of the year (when it is much less common in Singapore) are visitors from the south. Identification is fairly easy. It is medium sized, with a white head and underparts, a conspicuous black stripe through the eye and a brown breast band. In flight the black carpal patches can be seen and the wings are angled at the wrist, giving them a rather droopy appearance. The head appears small and often angled upwards. In hunting it will locate a fish in the water then plunge down from a great height with the wings held back and feet thrust forward. Disappearing in a cloud of spray it will then flap upwards, heavily if its catch is big. In locating prey it will sometimes hover for a few seconds before diving. The feet are equipped with special rough scales to facilitate gripping a slippery fish, and have two toes pointing forwards and two back. When flying off with prey the fish is always held in a "fore-and-aft" position, along the axis of the bird's body. It is usually seen hunting around the coastline, and often sits on the stakes of *kelongs* to rest, but may also fish over reservoirs.

13. BLACK BAZA (*Aviceda leuphotes*) (13″/33cm)

A winter visitor to Singapore in small numbers. The usual view is of a small, dark bird of prey with a very flappy wingbeat reminiscent of a crow. They have rather gregarious habits, somewhat unusual in birds of prey. They will roost in small groups and up to ten or twelve of them may be seen at dusk flying together to a roost site. It is very likely that many of these flocks are dismissed as crows. At rest the beautiful markings of the breast and the prominent crest can be seen. The white markings on the upper surface of the wing are very variable in location and extent, but whether they are of significance in determining the sex or race I do not know. In Singapore they will roost in the catchment area, mangroves or groups of tall trees in agricultural areas. Their food usually consists of insects, but they are also known to take frogs, lizards and small mammals.

14. BLACK-SHOULDERED KITE *(Elanus caeruleus)* (13"/33cm)

This is arguably our most beautiful raptor, the sleek grey and black plumage being complemented by a bright red eye giving it a suitably fierce look. This, coupled with its small size, makes it easily identified. In flight the wings are quite pointed, rather like a falcon, and the tail looks relatively short. It is the only one of our raptors to be seen hovering whilst looking for prey. (N.B. The very much larger and rarer Short-toed Eagle will also hover). The usual hunting technique is rapid flight, often at low levels, interspersed with hovering and diving onto prey. Items taken vary from small mammals and birds to insects. They seem to become attached to certain areas and can often be seen using regular perches. In Singapore they are usually associated with areas of rank grass and scrubby vegetation — old estates and vacant land behind mangroves. They can occur close to habitation and we have had reports of pairs displaying and talon-grappling over fields near Ang Mo Kio. Early works on Singapore did not refer to this species and it was first recorded only in the early 1930s, as a non-breeding visitor. They now seem to be fully resident, although I do not know of any confirmed records of nesting. This change in status has paralleled a similar increase in numbers in the Malay Peninsula.

59

15. EURASIAN HONEY-BUZZARD
(*Pernis apivorus*)   (20"/51cm)

In the Malay Peninsula there are two sub-species of this bird recorded: one (*torquatus*) is present throughout the year and, from the young birds which have been collected, is presumed to be resident. The other (*orientalis*) occurs as a passage migrant. Honey Buzzards are only seen in Singapore during migration and in winter, and so we assume that these are the latter sub-species. On migration they can regularly occur in flocks and large numbers can occasionally be seen soaring in thermals in the later morning just as the hot air begins to rise. Their main migration route down the peninsula follows the western coastal plain. Large numbers pass over this each year; counts in Selangor some years ago estimated 180,000 passing over during a 4½ week period (Medway and Wells). But most of these seem to pass over the Malacca Straits at Cape Rachado so our Singapore sightings probably never reach these numbers. The plumage of this bird is very variable and it can occur in light forms and dark forms with various intermediates. Throughout these forms there are several features which aid in identification. It is usually seen soaring and the silhouette is distinctive: unlike other buzzards and eagles it has a small head, set onto a slender neck, and the tail is rather long and usually held closed (not fanned). These two features contrive to give the bird a somewhat sleek, elongated appearance. The pattern of dark bands on the tail (two narrow near the base and one which is broader at the tip) is peculiar to this species and shown by almost all the plumages, with the exception of the immatures where the bands are narrower and more evenly spaced. This same banded pattern is also repeated on the wings but is sometimes harder to see. As the name suggests, it does attack bee and wasp nests (as well as hornets) where it eats the larvae and pupae and probably also the honey and comb. It has tiny scale-like feathers on the face, presumably to protect it from stings. Other adaptations for digging into wasp nests include strong feet with very thick scales and sharp, slightly curved claws. They also have slit-like nostrils to prevent clogging by debris. It also takes on a wide variety of other prey including birds, insects, reptiles and mammals. I have heard of 'eagles' attacking wasp nests in Singapore but have never been able to determine if it really was this species.

16. BRAHMINY KITE *(Haliastur indus)* (18"/46cm)

This is our most familiar bird of prey, the chestnut and white plumage preventing confusion with any other species. It is sometimes erroneously referred to as a sea eagle, a larger species in which the chestnut is replaced with grey. It is most commonly seen around the coastlines where it continuously soars and circles in search of food. It is predominantly a scavenger and for this reason is plentiful in the harbour areas and anchorages where edible waste thrown overboard makes easy pickings. When the opportunity arises they will also take fish, crabs, insects and even rats. They can be seen coursing over the larger rivers and canals well into the centre of the island and will hunt over parks and green open spaces. They usually nest in mangroves, and perhaps still do on larger offshore islands, but on the main island they prefer casuarinas near the coast although there are reports of them breeding as far inland as Balmoral Road. The immature birds are a dull brown colour with patches and streaks of buff and dark brown. In flight they show a pale patch on the underside of the primary feathers. The call note is a nasal, drawn out, plaintive "kweeaa".

imm.

imm.

17

JARVIS.

17. WHITE-BELLIED SEA-EAGLE *(Haliaeetus leucogaster)* (28"/71cm)

Our largest and most magnificent bird of prey. In silhouette the large size and wedge-shaped tail identify it. When colours can be seen the plumage pattern is similar to that of the Brahminy Kite, but the white extends down over the belly and onto the wings and tail and the chestnut is replaced by steel grey. The immatures are a blotchy brown colour. They have a heavy flapping flight and, like many large birds, resort to soaring and gliding to save energy; they do this with the wings held in a shallow "V". They can be seen all around the coastline, on offshore islands and by the reservoirs in the catchment area. They will catch fish and sea-snakes by making long, shallow glides over the surface of the water and picking off those close to the surface. They do not plunge vertically in the manner of an Osprey. Although nesting near the coast, most of our pairs seem to breed either on off-shore islands or in the forests of the catchment area — the latter area being ideal, with many tall trees overlooking water well-stocked with fish. Older texts refer to them nesting in the Botanic Gardens and elsewhere in the Tanglin district, although none seem to do so now. Nest sites are used for many years, the nest being added to each year until it grows into a massive pile of sticks. They have a characteristic honking cry, usually heard at dawn and dusk. They spend a large part of the day on high perches and are fond of the radio masts at Kranji and Bukit Timah Hill. Sometimes up to six or eight can be seen circling together at dusk.

18. JAPANESE SPARROWHAWK *(Accipiter gularis)* (11"/28cm)

This small hawk is a passage migrant and winter visitor to Singapore. It has a long tail and rather rounded wings. In adult plumage the male is grey-brown above with a belly which is actually covered in very fine rufous bars. The female is larger, more brown above than the male with white and grey barring on the breast and belly. Both sexes have bold bars on the underside of the wings and tail. Considerable variations can occur in the plumage, especially that of the juveniles which have pale-edged feathers and spots. They will migrate in large flocks, soaring very high, often in the company of other migrating raptors. When hunting they will progress in a series of circles with the characteristic "flap-flap glide" flight of sparrowhawks. Their usual food is small birds, and they can be seen chasing munias and bulbuls, but have been known to kill birds as large as a Spotted-necked Dove. I have seen them suddenly dash into an area where they seem to know that prey may be located, following, for example, a line of bushes and pouncing over the top on to a flock of sparrows. It is possible that they may have regular winter hunting territories and may learn the habits of the prey within it. Like many birds of prey, sparrowhawks will cause a sudden panic amongst smaller birds, long before they are visible to humans — a clue for the birdwatcher to be on guard for a sudden appearance.

♂

♀

JARVIS.

19. WHITE-BREASTED WATERHEN *(Amaurornis phoenicurus)* (13"/33cm)

The contrast between the white face and breast and the dark wings and back are distinctive. Confusion could only arise with the Pheasant-tailed Jacana which is a more colourful bird, shows more white, especially on the wings in flight, has a very long tail in breeding plumage and is a rare winter visitor to Singapore. The White-breasted Waterhen is very common anywhere near dense undergrowth, especially if water is nearby. It can be found in gardens and will often "commute" through suburban areas by sneaking along monsoon drains. It tends to be very shy and secretive and is easily overlooked. When driving through the farming areas of Mandai and Seletar it can often be seen on the road, diving into the long grass at the edge as you approach. When relaxed it will strut along with the tail cocked up, giving it an occasional flick; when alarmed the head will go down and it will make a headlong charge for cover, sometimes running up and down in a most panic-stricken manner. Whilst feeding it

64

20 ♂

♀/imm.

will strut with the feet lifted high, pecking at the ground like a chicken, so that it is sometimes called "*ayam-ayam*". It is usually seen on the ground but will also clamber around clumsily in bushes. If caught by surprise it may sometimes leap into water where it swims poorly. Or it may be forced into a tree where the long toes become a distinct handicap. It has a remarkable vocal repertoire: the traditional Malay name of "*uwak-uwak*" is a rendering of a monotonous call given at dawn and dusk. A whole host of churrs, grunts and groans are also made and it will sometimes call after dark. Other members of the rail family have been shown to have very interesting courtship displays when calling, but this bird only calls from the most dense cover and it is almost impossible to observe its activities. Juvenile birds are grey-brown all over. A different sub-species occurs on migration but cannot be separated in the field. Breeding may occur in any month of the year.

20. WATERCOCK *(Gallicrex cinerea)* (17"/44cm)

This is a very difficult bird to get good views of due to its habit of staying in dense cover in long grass and swampy areas. It is seldom recorded far from water and the usual view is of a large bird, mottled brown in colour, flying over the top of the marsh with rapidly flapping wings and long legs trailing behind. It appears to be a winter visitor to Singapore but we now have several records from the middle months of the year. The birds we usually see are brown, which could either be winter plumage males or females. In breeding plumage the males turn black and develop a fleshy horn over the beak. I have not seen a male in breeding plumage in Singapore, neither do we have any nesting records. The best place to find it is in the marsh areas around the edge of Kranji reservoir. It is recorded as having a call which is a popping and booming sound, similar in quality to that of a coucal.

21. PURPLE SWAMPHEN *(Porphyrio porphyrio)* (17"/43cm)

Superficially this is like the Moorhen but it is very much larger, the plumage is a glossy greenish-blue, and it has a huge red beak. Numbers seem to have increased in Singapore in recent years but it is very local in its distribution, fairly common at Kranji but recorded from only two or three other locations. Even at Kranji it is not as common as the Moorhen. Again, it is never found far from water and usually prefers to stay in dense cover in rank vegetation and floating weeds. It can hide surprisingly well considering its bulk and is difficult to flush. Unlike the Moorhen it will not swim or walk over open areas. The rafts of Water Hyacinth which cover the reservoirs give it ideal cover: the long toes spread the weight over a large area and allow it to walk on floating vegetation. When in flight it appears as a large bird with ponderous wing movements, the long red legs trailing behind. The diet is mostly water-weeds and other vegetable matter, and it has been known to cause damage to crop seedlings. Observations on captive individuals show that they will hold dead fish under a foot and chop off pieces. It usually feeds whilst on foot. It is recorded as making a range of typical rail-type squawks but the sound I usually associate with it is a nasal trumpeting "waak" which can carry for a long distance over water. The breeding behaviour is not fully understood. In some places it forms monogamous pairs whilst in others apparently co-operative breeding groups have been formed. At a distance its presence is often betrayed by an outstretched wing, but whether this is a display or sunbathing I am not sure.

22. COMMON MOORHEN *(Gallinula chloropus)* (13"/33cm)

The generally bronzish appearance with red bill and shield is distinctive. Early in the year they may look quite glossy but as the plumage becomes worn they take on a dusty appearance and the white flank-line may almost disappear. The juvenile plumage is generally dark brown, paler below. They have an olive beak with no shield which gives them a much more pointed appearance than the adults. This is the original "clockwork bird"; when swimming the head jerks with every push of the feet, whilst on land it moves with a very high-stepping gait with the tail held high and constantly flicking. It is never found away from water and in Singapore seems to be fond of those reservoirs formed by damming the mouth of a river, hence such places as Kranji and the west coast area are its favourite haunts. It may also be seen in the catchment area and around the edge of rivers leading into mangroves. They will leave the water to graze on grass but usually keep near to cover. In fact they are probably the easiest of our rails to see and will grow accustomed to human presence. They can occasionally be found in trees and have been known to nest there. They fly well, as is perhaps illustrated by their abilities to colonise new areas. It has a wide distribution in South-east Asia but is only ever locally common. It seems to be increasing in numbers in Singapore. They form territories during the breeding season and have a whole host of interesting displays to defend them. One of the display postures is to flash the white undertail coverts at each other. They are omnivorous and eat a wide variety of plant and animal material. They will feed on land by pecking, or whilst swimming by dipping the head under water. Very occasionally they can be seen up-ending to pick at something deeper in the water. The call is a loud, harsh "kurruk".

21

22

23. GREY PLOVER (*Pluvialis squatarola*) (11"/28cm)

Of the two larger plovers in Singapore this is the less common. At a distance in winter plumage is told only with some difficulty from the slightly smaller **Pacific Golden Plover.** In good light, however, it does appear a definite grey-colour on the back and paler underneath. In flight it is told from all other waders by the black patch where the underside of the wing joins the body (axillaries), and when seen from above has a white (or near white) rump. It appears to favour sandy coastlines and can usually be seen in the Changi area, never inland. Its call is a very mournful "tleeuoo-wee", rather slurred and descending in the middle. It usually occurs in flocks (as do all the winter waders here), but only of around 10–2 birds. It never reaches the large numbers of some of the other waders, and does not appear to migrate in large flocks. When feeding they are well spaced out and if one bird is watched it will walk a few paces, stop, peck, walk, stop, peck, stop, etc so that most of the time they appear to be standing still.

23 winter

24

24 winter

24. PACIFIC GOLDEN PLOVER *(Pluvialis fulva)* (10"/25cm)

Smaller than the Grey Plover, in Singapore it is much more common and is perhaps the most numerous of the waders. In places such as the Serangoon estuary it attains very large numbers. It migrates in large flocks and these flocks seem to stay together for feeding and roosting. They will feed on short grass, as well as the mudflats, and can sometimes be seen a long way from the coast. One such favourite haunt is the rather wet playing fields of the Institute of Education along Bukit Timah Road. They may also be found on the shores of the reservoirs in the catchment area. They feed in the same manner as the Grey but are usually in larger flocks and spaced more closely together. When they first arrive in September/October, and again before departing in April, many may be seen in their breeding plumage.

The jet black breast and face give it a splendid appearance. Small numbers may be seen after April and there are records from just about every month; there is no evidence yet to suggest that any individuals spend the whole year here. The call is a disyllabic "klee-eet", less plaintive than the Grey, perhaps better rendered by the Malay name *"keriyut"*.

24 summer

23 summer

JARVIS.

25. LITTLE RINGED PLOVER *(Charadrius dubius)* (7"/18cm)

This is the most numerous of the small plovers which visit Singapore. These can be difficult for the beginner to identify and so some discussion of their characteristics is worthwhile. In breeding plumage look for the combination of a dark breast-band, white collar, black face and yellow eye-ring. The very rare Ringed Plover is one inch bigger and lacks the extra white band on the forehead above the eye; it also has an orange beak and the legs are orange not yellow. The Ringed Plover has a wing bar in flight whereas the Little Ringed does not. We also have the Kentish Plover which does not have a complete breast band and tends to look rather bull-headed. In winter plumage the black areas of the Little Ringed go brown but the eye-ring is still distinctive. At this time we also see a lot of juveniles which have a broken breast band and a brown hood; this invites confusion with the Kentish which in winter looks a very white bird. The only other small plover entering into this confusion is the Malaysian Sand Plover, a solitary bird which breeds on the sandy East Coast of Malaysia and may be breeding in Singapore. This has a broad black band around the back of the neck, a black shoulder patch (not breast band) and a black mark on the forehead separated from one behind the eye. The Little

Ringed Plover feeds in a characteristic stop-run-peck manner, usually higher up the shore on drier sand or mud. It often can be seen "pattering" — standing on one leg whilst rapidly vibrating the other on the surface of the sand or mud, usually running forward to peck at something after doing this for a few seconds Presumably this action somehow disturbs thei invertebrate prey and causes them to move, thereby betraying their position. Although only a winter visitor to Singapore they have been recorded as early as the end of July. In flight it has a single clear "teeuu" call.

26

25

26 summer

winter

25

Definitive Features of Small Plovers

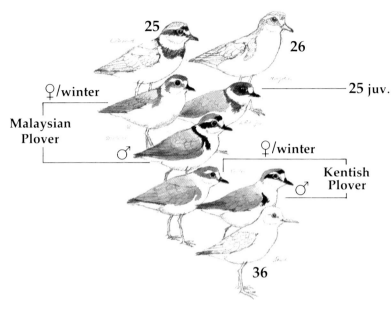

25

26

♀/winter

Malaysian
Plover

25 juv.

♂

♀/winter

Kentish
Plover

♂

36

IN SUMMER (BREEDING) PLUMAGE

1. Little Ringed Plover		Complete black breast band, orange-yellow legs, yellow eyering.
2. Kentish Plover	m.	Sandy rufous cap, black side patch with no black behind neck.
	f.	As male but black replaced by brown.
3. Malaysian Plover	m.	Sandy rufous cap, black side patch which extends into a collar behind neck.
	f.	As male but black replaced by brown.
4. Mongolian Plover		Black mask, rufous breast band, no white collar behind neck.

IN WINTER (NON-BREEDING) AND IMMATURE PLUMAGE

1. Little Ringed Plover	ad.wint.	Black areas go dark brown.
	imm.	All brown head with no white markings, brown breast band broken in the middle.
2. Kentish Plover	ad.wint.	Black areas go brown.
	imm.	As adult winter but slightly greyer in colour.
3. Malaysian Plover	ad.wint.	Black areas go dark brown.
	imm.	Like female but without sandy cap.
4. Mongolian Plover	ad.wint.	White forehead and eyebrow, brown side patch.
	imm.	As adults.

m. = male: f = female; ad.wint. = adult winter; imm. = immature

27

28

JARVIS.

26. MONGOLIAN PLOVER *(Charadrius mongolus)*   (8"/20cm)

This bird is larger than the preceding species and lacks a white collar. In summer it has a rufous breast-band and black mask, and in winter has a white forehead and eyebrow, and a brown shoulder patch. It could only be confused with the Greater Sand Plover, which in Singapore seems quite rare, but in fairness can only be told with great difficulty by its heavier bill and slightly longer legs. Although it associates with all the other waders it seems to form loose flocks, with individuals well separated from each other.

27. WHIMBREL *(Numenius phaeopus)*   (17"/43cm)

We have only two common large waders with long decurved beaks, this and the much larger Curlew. The latter is less common in Singapore, occurring only in singles or twos and very infrequently. The Whimbrel has a dark cap and a pale stripe above the eye. It has a proportionately shorter bill than the Curlew and it seems to be flat close to the head, turning down about half way along. In flight the Whimbrel has a pale rump extending in a triangle up the back; in the Curlew it is pure white. It is usually seen in flocks of from five to 30, never in large numbers; when feeding on the mud the flock becomes spread out. It never appears to probe deeply in the mud despite having the apparatus to do so. In India it is recorded as dragging fiddler crabs from their burrows, pulling off the fiddle and swallowing the rest whole. It gives the descending tittering trill typical of these birds but a harsh squawk is more common when alarmed. Another early arrival, sometimes found in July.

28. BLACK-TAILED GODWIT *(Limosa limosa)*   (16"/41cm)

Of the two Godwits recorded from Singapore this is by far the more common, the Bar-tailed Godwit occurring usually as single birds and not in every year. At rest the two are separated only with difficulty, the Black-tailed having a longer, straighter bill. In flight they are easily separated since the Black-tailed has a conspicuous white wing bar, and a white tail with a broad black band across the tip. It is a stately looking bird and, although large, has none of the ungainly manner or appearance of the Whimbrel. Early arriving and late leaving birds may be seen in their summer plumage, which assumes a lovely pink-chestnut colour on the head, neck and breast, fainter and with dark bars on the belly. They usually stay together in flocks. One, of about 160, which wintered in the Serangoon Estuary habitually fed together and roosted on the same spit of land. It feeds by probing deeply, the bird often pivoting around in circles as if unscrewing its prey from the mud! The call is a thrice-repeated "wicka-wicka-wicka". It is worth looking carefully at Godwit flocks for the rare Asian Dowitcher, told by its larger size and very long, entirely black beak.

29. MARSH SANDPIPER *(Tringa stagnatilis)* (10″/25cm)

This is one of the most elegant of waders, rather like a miniature Greenshank and easily mistaken for that species when alone. It has a more slender build, however, and the bill is proportionately shorter, straighter and more slender whilst the legs are proportionately longer. It usually occurs singly but in a suitable feeding site several birds may be gathered together. Although showing a preference for fresh-water feeding it will join the other birds on the mudflats. It may be seen along river banks, in flooded fields and the evaporation beds of sewage works. It will wade up to its belly in water, sweeping around with its beak for prey. In the 1930s it was regarded as a very rare bird but is now fairly common.

30. COMMON GREENSHANK *(Tringa nebularia)* (14"/36cm)

A medium-sized wader (mid-way between a Redshank and a Black-tailed Godwit), predominantly grey above. The underside is almost white, and the head, and to a lesser extent the breast, is streaked with dark grey. The tail and rump are white, the former barred slightly. The legs are greenish; the bill appears rather stout and tends to curve up slightly. In flight both this and the Marsh Sandpiper show a long white triangle up the centre of the back. It is fairly common, mixing with other waders on the sea-shore and mudflats. It will also penetrate some distance inland and can be seen on the shores of the reservoirs of the catchment area. It is usually seen singly or in pairs but occasionally in flocks of up to 20 or 30 birds, individuals of which may be very spread out when feeding. It can be quite noisy and the call is a ringing "tchu-tchu-tchu", the syllable sometimes being repeated up to six times.

31. COMMON REDSHANK *(Tringa totanus)* (11"/28cm)

The name derives from old English meaning red legs, for obvious reasons. But beware of juvenile birds with greenish-yellow legs and adults with mud adhering to them. Although we have several different sub-species of this bird, all tend to be a fairly uniform grey-brown in winter with a noticeably darker head; the breast is streaked to varying degrees. In flight the white of the rump extends well up the back in a wedge shape, and the wings have a white trailing edge — a pattern shown only by this and the Terek Sandpiper. It is inevitably found in flocks and often in large numbers. Although muddy coastlines are favoured it will feed over a large range of substrates from the softest mud to sandy foreshores. The call is a clear whistled "teu hu-hu", the first note sliding down and the second two brief and on the same pitch. Also a longer whistled "teyuu" often used when alert or alarmed, at which time it will jerk its head and neck up and down. It seems to be generally noisier and more nervous than the other waders. At high tide it will often roost on old stumps and jetties, or in mangrove trees.

31

32

32. COMMON SANDPIPER *(Actitis hypoleucos)* (8"/20cm)

Occurring almost everywhere, on sea-shores, beaches, flooded fields and ditches, this little bird seems to be the least specialised of the waders. A plain grey-brown above, with a dark patch either side of the breast. In flight a white wing bar is conspicuous. It has a very characteristic stance — short-legged with the body tilted forwards, the tail bobbing up and down almost continuously. When it flies it does so with very stiff, shallow wingbeats; the wings never seem to come above the horizontal, and it will skim the surface of the water. It typically potters along the edge of the water, either singly or in pairs, working its way busily in and out. It is usually confiding, allowing one to approach fairly close before flying off a short distance. Individuals can be seen in every month and it is often erroneously assumed to breed here. In fact it is a passage migrant and winter visitor. Almost all the small waders are called *"kedidi"* in Malay, but the name probably originated with this species since this is an accurate rendition of its thin, high-pitched call.

33. TEREK SANDPIPER *(Xenus cinereus)* (10"/25cm)

At a glance this bird is rather reminiscent of the Common Sandpiper. It has short legs, plain grey upperparts and will bob the tail, although not quite so vigorously as the preceding species. However this is where the resemblance ends. The short legs are orange, the underparts white, and it is the only one of our waders to have a conspicuously upturned bill. In flight it has a white trailing edge to the wing like the Redshank. It will form small flocks and is usually seen in the company of other waders feeding on soft mud. It will walk around very quickly and seems in constant danger of toppling over. It feeds by walking with the head down, probing from side to side. Larger items are sometimes washed before swallowing with an upward flick of the head.

34. WOOD SANDPIPER *(Tringa glareola)*

A very common winter visitor which prefers fresh-water areas to the sea-shore. It can be found on the shore with other waders but is usually on the very edge and near the river mouths etc. It also favours quite narrow rivers, flooded fields and wasteland. It is a bird which seems to lack any conspicuous characteristics for identification. The legs are greenish-yellow and the upper parts seem very scaly with grey/buff spots on a grey/brown background. It also has a darkish cap to the head and a white line above the eye, but none of these characteristics are very bold.
In flight the dark back squarely cut off from the white upper tail coverts separates it from some of the other common waders. It is always rather timid and is very often the first bird to fly off, sounding the alarm with a high pitched "chip-yip-yip", a call similar to, but lacking the ring of, a Greenshank.

34

33

77

JARVIS.

35. PINTAIL SNIPE *(Gallinago stenura)* (10"/25cm)

Snipe were first known in this region as the favoured bird of "sportsmen" with their shotguns. When reading of the numbers which could be shot at one time it is clear that the species is now very much reduced, but probably more by habitat loss than by hunting. They favour low-lying, boggy ground, especially where there are bushes and rank grass. The draining of this type of land in Singapore (and elsewhere) has drastically reduced the amount of available habitat. Such was the popularity of snipe shooting that Bucknill and Chasen make reference to a large Singapore firm which used to maintain its own snipe marsh "just beyond the village of Paya Lebar". It is mainly due to the sportsman's bag that we know something of the status of our snipe, because all are extremely difficult to identify in the field. There are four species recorded from Singapore, although the Wood Snipe by only one specimen (Gibson-Hill 1956). Of the remaining three the most

common is the Pintail Snipe, so called because the outer seven or eight tail feathers are stiff and narrow, not soft as normal. The Common (or Fantail) Snipe and Swinhoe's Snipe also occur, but in much smaller numbers (see Medway and Wells for an idea of proportions). The Common Snipe has a white trailing edge to the inner part of the wing, visible to the sharp observer as the bird flies away; it has an erratic zig-zag flight when flushed. The Pintail and Swinhoe's both lack any white in the wing and there seems no obvious way of separating them in the field. All the birds fly off low, uttering a call "scaap" or "zaak", the call of the Pintail being higher in pitch than the Common. Often they will hunch down in the grass, allowing a very close approach; as soon as one bird panics and flies off a dozen or more may rise over a small area. At a distance they are easily told from the other waders by the mottled appearance, very long bill, short legs and striped head. Will form large flocks.

78

36. RUFOUS-NECKED STINT *(Calidris ruficollis)* (6.5"/17cm)

The stints are small, sparrow-sized waders with a correspondingly dumpy appearance. In certain parts of the world, where several species occur together, they create great problems of identification for birdwatchers. In Singapore our two common species are fairly easily separated. Contrary to the image suggested, the Red-necked Stint is the paler of the two in winter plumage. The upper parts are a plain grey colour, whilst the underparts are creamy white. The legs are a very dark olive, almost black, the bill is short and black. In summer plumage the face and neck assume a nice pink-red colour; a hint of this can be seen in some of the birds in March but we rarely see anything approaching the full nuptial plumage. They feed with a busy probing action and can sometimes be found feeding in fresh-water.

37. LONG-TOED STINT *(Calidris subminuta)* (6.5"/17cm)

Found in large flocks along with the Red-necked Stint, but probably in smaller numbers. The upperparts are brown scaled with black, very reminiscent of the colouring of a snipe. The neck has a band of brown streaks across it and the legs are yellow. The short black bill has a slight decurve to it. It feeds with a more leisurely action than the Red-necked Stint. They are found feeding on the softer mud of the coasts, always in flocks which sweep and wheel around as the tide changes. There is one other stint recorded from Singapore — Temminck's Stint. Like the Long-toed it too has yellow legs, but the breast is unstreaked and the back is a plain dull brown-grey colour. It is habitually a solitary bird, to be found in fresh-water marshes and is somewhat uncommon in Singapore.

37

37

36

JARVIS

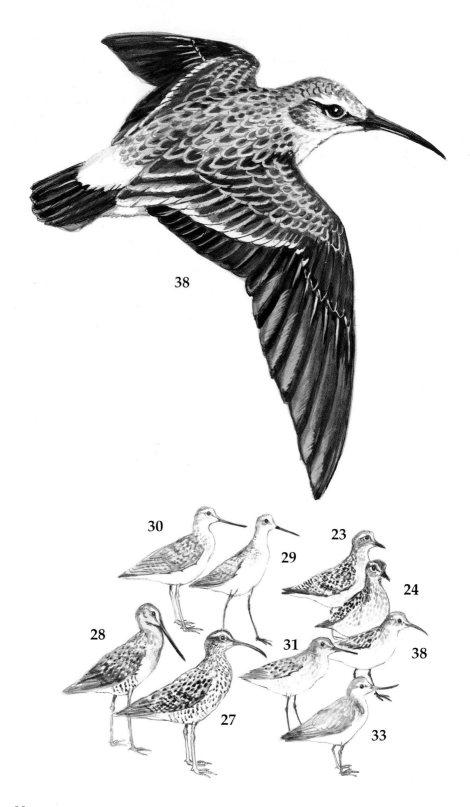

38

30
29
23
24
28
31
38
27
33

38. CURLEW SANDPIPER *(Calidris ferruginea)*   (8.5″/22cm)

This bird is intermediate in size, between the stints and the Redshank, and usually occurs in large flocks. As the name suggests this bird has a down-curved beak, our only small wader to have this. The plumage is a plain grey colour, white underneath with a grey wash on the breast, and white eyebrow. In flight it is the only one of the small waders with a completely white rump. In summer the face, breast and belly assume a deep rufous colour of the tone of the Black-tailed Godwit; this may be seen in some of the early arrivals in August and also in March/April before departure. It usually feeds in large flocks which often associate with the stints. Seen on muddy shores and prawn ponds. It undertakes long migrations. It breeds on the northern coast of Russia and will fly to southern Australia to winter.

39. ORIENTAL PRATINCOLE *(Glareola maldivarum)* (10"/25cm)

Although closely related to the waders, this is a bird of very different appearance and habits. The short legs, wide short beak, forked tail and swept-back wings are consistent with their habits of feeding on the wing, swooping and diving after insects just like swallows. The rather large size and forked tail also make them appear like terns in flight. They seem to spend most of the hot part of the day on the ground, preferring dry, bare terrain, or short grass; the brown and black upperparts render them almost invisible against such backgrounds. This habit also causes them to be a hazard at airports since large flocks may be attracted to the short grass of the aprons.

They seem to occur mainly in flocks (of up to 200 birds), usually during the passage periods of October/November and February/March. They breed in the northern states of the Malay Peninsula but are migrants in Singapore. They have a coarse, tern-like call.

39

40. GREAT CRESTED TERN *(Sterna bergii)*   (18"/46cm)

This bird can be seen in almost every month of the year, but on present evidence it does not breed south of Thailand. It is the largest common tern in Singapore waters, the greenish-yellow bill, black crest and long forked tail identifying it. It can often be seen around Changi, resting on sand bars where it towers over the Little Terns which share this habit. We also get in smaller numbers the Lesser Crested Tern, which is a smaller bird; in summer the bill is bright orange-yellow and there is no white on the forehead; in winter almost the entire crown becomes white. The Great Crested Tern is usually seen away from the coast, fishing in deeper, clearer waters. They will often land on the stakes of the *kelongs* to rest; scanning those in the Straits of Johore in winter will inevitably reveal several.

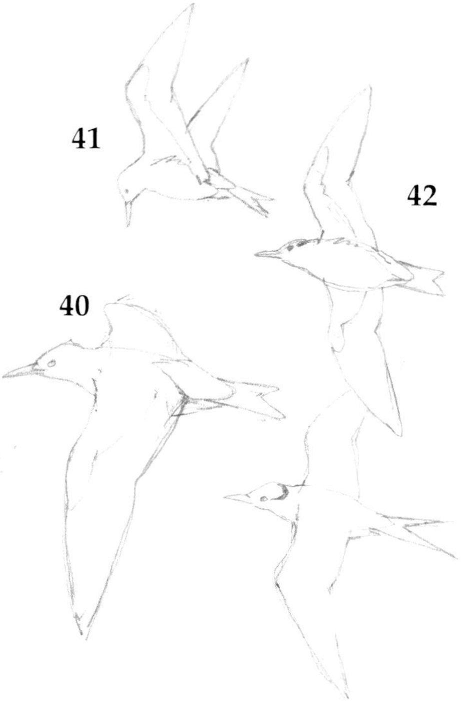

41

42

40

Black-naped Tern
(Sterna sumatrana)

40

83

41 winter

summer

42 winter

summer

JARVIS.

41. LITTLE TERN *(Sterna albifrons)*

Based on present evidence this bird seems to be a winter visitor to Singapore, although breeding has been recorded only 200 miles north of here, and birds in breeding plumage are occasionally seen in Singapore. As the name suggests it is our smallest tern and this, coupled with rapid, stiff wingbeats, is its main identifying feature. It also has a habit of flying along with its beak pointing vertically down at the water as it searches for fish. When the latter are spotted it can turn and dive with great rapidity rather than hovering as other terns will do. In breeding plumage the beak is yellow with a black tip. In winter the leading edge of the wing is dark grey to the tips of the primaries, giving the impression of a dark, inverted "W" when in flight. It may be seen all around the coast, usually close in where it seems to prefer muddy waters, and occasionally on the inland reservoirs; at Kranji they pass back and forth regularly over the dam. It is another species which was once regarded as rare in Singapore but it is more likely to have been overlooked.

41 winter

summer

42 winter

42. WHITE-WINGED TERN
(Chlidonias leucopterus) (10"/26cm)

This bird undergoes a remarkable change in its plumage during the year and we are lucky enough to see both forms. It is a winter visitor and when the first birds arrive in October/ November they are usually already in their winter plumage. This is generally grey, white underneath, with a black crown and ear patch, and the forehead is white. They stay this way until April when, just before departing for their breeding grounds, the entire head, body and underwing coverts go jet black, and as they depart all birds seem to be in this nuptial plumage. They are more common at the beginning and end of the above period and are found all around the coastline and sometimes on the fresh-water reservoirs, usually in flocks. They have a buoyant flight and tend to feed by dipping to the water's surface rather than plunge diving.

summer

43 ♀

43 ♂

43. PINK-NECKED PIGEON *(Treron vernans)* (10.5"/27cm)

This is the only common green pigeon in Singapore and the only one to be seen away from the forest. They occur commonly in parks and gardens, mangrove and the forest, often in flocks of anything up to 30 birds at a time. Their food seems to be exclusively fruit and they will frequent a fruiting fig or other tree regularly until the food is exhausted. They are also fond of the fruits of the Tembusu, various palms and will come down low to the Straits Rhododendron. When high in the canopy their colour makes them difficult to see in the foliage. Roosting communally they can sometimes be seen flying between fruiting tree and roost site in the morning and evening, although this behaviour seems to be less common in Singapore than has been recorded elsewhere. The nest is usually built low down; I have seen several in the larger bougainvillaeas in the Botanic Gardens. Like most pigeons, a very flimsy platform is constructed about 15–20 cm in diameter, between two and 10 metres above the ground, and very often the contents can be assessed by looking through the holes in the base! The voice is a peculiar bubbling, squeaking "ooo-ooo, cheweeo-cheweeoo-cheweeoo" followed by two or three harsh rasping noises, with the bird often hidden.

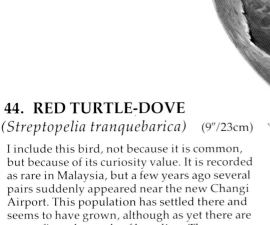

44. RED TURTLE-DOVE
(Streptopelia tranquebarica) (9"/23cm)

I include this bird, not because it is common, but because of its curiosity value. It is recorded as rare in Malaysia, but a few years ago several pairs suddenly appeared near the new Changi Airport. This population has settled there and seems to have grown, although as yet there are no confirmed records of breeding. They seem to like the open country around that region and can be easily seen loafing on the tall perimeter fence of the airport. The nearest natural population is in Thailand and it has occasionally been seen in Malaysia. It is tempting to think in terms of an expansion of range, but escapes from the bird trade have been recorded in Singapore earlier this century and this seems the more likely reason for its current occurrence here. The population now seems well entrenched and time will tell whether they spread to other parts of the island. It seems likely that they will.

45. SPOTTED DOVE *(Streptopelia chinensis)* (12″/30cm)

This is one of only two brown pigeons in Singapore, its size and distinct spotted collar being diagnostic. In flight it appears to have a long tail and it gives a noisy clapping of the wings as it takes off. The clapping of the wings is also noticeable when the bird gives its display flight, whereby a series of hard flaps causes it to rise very steeply, after which it swoops down in a circular glide when it gives the brief impression of a sparrowhawk. The Malay name of *"tekukor"* is a rendering of the somewhat monotonous song. It can be found almost everywhere on the island but is most common in the more rural areas and on wasteland. Although found on the edge of the forest it does not venture inside. Taking grass seeds, which it picks from the ground, it is most often seen feeding on short grass and lawns — especially if there is longer grass nearby which has been allowed to seed. The rather flimsy nest is often built in very exposed places in low trees or tall bushes. It is a very popular cage bird and wild ones are trapped in the quieter areas of the island. The principal method of trapping is to place a decoy bird in a small cage on the ground. Around the decoy is placed a string of 30–40 snares made from monofilament fishing line. Wild birds attracted by the singing of the decoy are caught by the legs in the snares when they alight.

46. PEACEFUL DOVE
(Geopelia striata) (8.5″/22cm)

A prettily-coloured dove with a blue-grey face, pinkish-buff undersides with the belly and flanks barred. It is altogether much smaller than the preceding species, and of a more delicate appearance. More shy than the Spotted-necked Dove, it is seldom seen in built-up areas, preferring the rural farming areas and forest edges; it seems to be fond of coconut trees and can often be heard singing from these. It feeds on grass seeds and can be seen picking at these on bare ground or short grass. It will usually feed near the trees or bushes into which it will quickly fly if threatened. They are strong fliers and there is some evidence they undergo dispersal flights: one bird ringed in Singapore in 1965 was recovered two years later 300 miles north in Cameron Highlands. The song is a rolling whistled "coo", usually repeated six to eight times. This rather unremarkable song has made it the subject of much big business because it is one of the favoured birds of the bird singing contests, champion singers changing hands for many thousands of dollars. Large numbers are illegally trapped and this, plus loss of long-grass habitats, may account for an apparent decline in its population size over recent years. I am told that very rarely do these wild caught birds produce good champions but are better used as breeding stock. The Malay name *"merbok"*, often used for the Spotted-necked Dove, is more correctly applied to this species.

47 ♂

47 ♀

JARVIS.

♂

47. LONG-TAILED PARAKEET
(Psittacula longicauda) (16"/41cm)

Most people express some surprise at being
told there are wild parrots in Singapore. But
this bird is not uncommon when one learns the
signs: it is most often seen flying high
overhead when its squawking flight call is the
first thing to draw your attention. The flight is
swift and they look very sleek with swept-back
wings and long pointed tail. They seem to be
more common on the northern part of the
island and in the catchment area. For reasons I
have never understood I have quite often seen
them flying over Sembawang Park out to sea in
the direction of Malaysia, and so it seems likely
that birds will fly to and fro over the Johore
Straits. I have seen a pair nesting in a hole in a
tall dead tree to the north of the Mandai Road.
We have at least two other similar-looking
parrots in Singapore, the Rose-ringed and the
Red-breasted, both escapees from the cage bird
trade, and one should take care to observe
the patterning on any that are seen perched.

48. BANDED BAY CUCKOO *(Cuculus sonneratii)* (9"/23cm)

A fairly small cuckoo characterised by the fine wavy dark bars all over the body. The ground colour of the back is bronze and of the underside a very light buff. The sexes are alike. It may be found in a wide variety of habitats including the forest reserves, agricultural land, and mature gardens. They lay their eggs in the nests of other birds. Young birds of this species cannot be identified with certainty in the field, but the Pied Triller, Common Iora and Common Tailorbird have all been seen feeding young cuckoos which have been attributed to this species. It seems to be heard calling most often between March and May. Various calls have been described for this bird and two seem to be commonly used in Singapore: (1) a shrill four note whistle on a descending scale popularly described as "smoke yer-pep-per", the first note being the longest of the four; (2) a much slower, mournful, rising sequence of "tee-too-taa-tay" repeated three or four times, each time at a higher pitch than the previous. This call often ends with a bubbling chatter.

49. MALAYAN BRONZE CUCKOO
(Chrysococcyx minutillus (malayanus))
(6.25"/16cm)

A very small cuckoo easily overlooked. In Singapore it can be found in the open country, mangrove edge, parks and gardens, usually fairly low down in the trees. It has a rather pale face, bronze back and faint barrings underneath. The orange eye-ring (the colour is difficult to see) gives it a wide-eyed appearance. It is very easily confused with an immature Pied Triller. It gives a very gentle call, similar to the "smoke-yer-pep-per" of the Banded Bay Cuckoo, but of a more reedy, trembling nature, and rather slower in tempo. It also has a long, high-pitched, descending trill. Flyeaters have been observed feeding young cuckoos thought to belong to this species. In practice young cuckoos are hard to identify and further research is required before we can be sure of the host species.

50. PLAINTIVE CUCKOO *(Cuculus merulinus)*

The colour patterning of the adults prevents confusion with any species other than the Brush Cuckoo, which in Singapore is very rare. The immature is hard to distinguish from the adult Banded Bay Cuckoo. It lays its eggs in the nest of other birds and this, coupled with its hawk-like profile, means it is often mobbed by smaller birds, especially during the breeding season. It has been reported as parasitising the nest of Tailor-birds and Ioras. Although occasionally found in forest it is most common in Singapore in open country, mangroves and cultivated land. Its occasional appearance in forest may be possible because of the absence of the Brush Cuckoo which replaces it in this habitat in the peninsula. The call notes are very distinctive and are often uttered from an exposed perch. Two commonly heard: (1) "tee-tar-tay" ("eat-more-froueet" — Glenister) with the middle note lower than the other two, repeated on a rising scale; (2) an accelerating, plaintive "pwee, pwee, pwee, pee-pee-pee-pee" on a descending scale. I have also heard it make a continuous downward series of "pui" notes almost identical to those of the Brush Cuckoo. Cuckoos often call at night, and the plaintive notes of this species, especially when present in gardens, led to the name "brain-fever bird", although this is also sometimes applied to some of the Hawk-cuckoos. The Malay name *"burong mati anak"* reflects the plaintive sobbing of the mourning for a dead child.

91

53

52 ad.

52 juv.

53

52

51. CHESTNUT-BELLIED MALKOHA *(Phaenicophaeus sumatranus)* (16"/41cm)

In the field the chestnut of the belly is often difficult to see, but it is the only malkoha found in Singapore and, although at one time it could be found in mangroves, it is now confined entirely to the forest of the central catchment area. Although members of the cuckoo family, malkohas do not lay their eggs in the nest of other birds; however a good description of the nest of this species does not seem to exist. It is usually encountered between the middle level and top of the canopy where it creeps about the foliage and creepers in a very cautious manner, moving rather slowly and staying still for long periods. In Singapore I have found this to be a rather silent bird but elsewhere I have heard it make a mewing call like a cat and a rather loud "tok" like a large hollow block of wood being struck by a stick. When it flies it does so rather weakly and is often seen gliding from the top of one tree to another. I have seen it eating large insects such as katydids and cicadas.

52. LESSER COUCAL *(Centropus bengalensis)* (15"/38cm)

The old name for the coucals was "crow-pheasant", which very aptly describes the appearance of these birds. They form another branch of the cuckoo family which does not parasitise the nests of other birds. This bird and the following species are not easily told apart, unless one is familiar with them, and this is complicated by the fact that they are both found in similar areas. The Lesser Coucal, as the name implies, is the smaller of the two and tends to have a more streaky, scruffy appearance in the field. This effect is due to the very glossy shafts of the head feathers which reflect light and appear almost white. It also has white streaks on the wings, mantle and breast. The immatures are basically buff and are heavily streaked all over with some barring on the wings and tail. The definitive characteristic of the adult is a chestnut wing lining, whereas the Greater Coucal has a black wing lining. In practice, however, I find that both birds always fly very low and seldom raise their wings above the horizontal. Whilst both species inhabit areas of long grass and scrub the Lesser Coucal seems to stay more in the grass itself, especially when it is tussocks of *lallang* intermingled with various herbs. It has a very strange call which is well-described by Medway and Wells as "a series of high-pitched hiccupping notes, 'hup, hup, hup ...' followed by a cackling 't-t-tok, t-tok ...'". This is usually made from a hidden perch.

53. GREATER COUCAL *(Centropus sinensis)* (21"/53cm)

Probably less common in Singapore than the preceding species, it is larger and more clumsy in appearance than the Lesser Coucal and the immature does not appear as streaky on the back, but has grey barrings on the breast and some black in the wings. The adult plumage has much deeper, richer colours than the Lesser. It prefers areas with low bushes and scrub, as well as grass, and can be found around the perimeter of old coconut estates and in the vegetable farming areas on the fringes of the fields. Both coucals feed off large insects, frogs and reptiles. They build bulky nests which are made of grass and are spherical with an entrance hole at the side: they are built within a foot or two of the ground. The call of the Greater Coucal is a series of slow, mournful notes "boop, boop, boop, boop ..." often on a descending scale and rather low in pitch. It often seems to call just before taking flight.

54. BARN OWL *(Tyto alba)* (13.5″/34cm)

This bird has undergone an amazing increase in population size in recent years. Although some of the earliest records of it came from Singapore it seems to have remained something of a rarity until recent times. In the Malay Peninsula it is closely associated with oil-palm estates and the rodent pests of these estates provide the rich food supply which has enabled a population increase to take place (Lenton 1982). In Singapore the number of records seems to increase each year. Sentosa Island has a small population, and although many other records come from the eastern, more rural side of the main island, there is a record of a pair breeding in the lift shaft of an HDB block in Queenstown. Thus a parallel increase seems to have occurred in Singapore, perhaps partly due to emigrants from the expanding population in Johore. The call is a hair-raising series of screeches and burbles, with a hissing sound made near the nest. It seems to be very shy in Singapore and is rarely seen hunting; my views of it have all been close to known nesting sites. With the heart-shaped facial disk and almost pure white underparts it is unlikely to be confused with any other species. The Bay Owl is a rare vagrant to Singapore. It has more rufous underparts and the facial disk is elongated into a pair of "ears".

JARVIS.

94

55. BROWN HAWK-OWL *(Ninox scutulata)* (12"/30cm)

Usually a bird of the forest areas, although in Malaysia it has been recorded from plantations and mangrove. It will occasionally visit gardens and I have twice seen it in this habitat, on both occasions fairly close to the Nature Reserves. Old records from the Botanic Gardens suggest that it was once more widespread on the island than it is today. Being a nocturnal forest bird, very little is known of its habits, although insects are said to feature prominently in the diet. I am told that the soles of the feet have small, sharp spines, similar to those found in piscivorous species, but I know of no records of this bird attempting to catch fish. The call is a strong, falsetto "hoo-up" which carries some distance. It appears to be more vocal around dawn and dusk. It will respond well to playback of recordings of its own voice and I have obtained good views of it this way.

JARVIS.

95

56. COLLARED SCOPS OWL
(*Otus bakkamoena*) (9"/23cm)

This small owl is a fairly common resident of virtually all our habitats, with the exception of mangroves. The plumage can be very variable: the ground colour can range from a pale sandy-buff to almost orange and the number and intensity of black markings are just as uncertain. Like all owls it is only seen with great difficulty. The easiest means of detecting its presence is to listen for its soft, disyllabic whistle "pee-oo" the second syllable of which is often difficult to detect so it sounds like a soft "pauk". It often seems to associate itself with the larger old colonial-style houses and I have seen it more than once roosting in the daytime in the garage or servants' quarters of these buildings. It is said to feed mostly on large beetles and other insects, but it is likely that other invertebrates and small vertebrates are also eaten. As with other birds of prey, the indigestible part of the diet is regurgitated as a "pellet".

57. LARGE-TAILED NIGHTJAR (*Caprimulgus macrurus*) (12"/30cm)

A familiar bird to just about everyone, by sound if not by sight. This is the bird which, from September to June, sits outside your bedroom window at night producing a monotonous "tok-tok-tok-tok", which makes it known in some parts as the tok-tok bird. More accurately the call is a rich, melodious "tchoink", like two large pebbles being struck together. It also makes a much quieter grunting noise like that of a frog croaking. This latter is made when two birds are in close proximity and could be related to the pair-bond, whereas the former is more likely to be a territorial call. They are nocturnal and insectivorous, catching their prey on the wing and often favouring a perch on service wires alongside a street light, from where they can fly out to catch the moths attracted to the light. In this position they are almost invisible since one is blinded by the light, but when they take flight the white patches on the wings and tail make a conspicuous flash in the darkness. They fly with a jerky, stiff winged action and glide with the wings raised above the body: this contrasts with the leisurely flap of an owl. They also have a habit of sitting on the road at night, their eyes shining in car headlights like red beacons. It is not clear why they do this, perhaps for the warmth of the tarmac. They are certainly often reluctant to rise and one can often see their squashed carcasses as a tribute to the speeds made available by the modern motor trade. They lay their eggs on the ground in a small depression, usually underneath a bush or a hedge. Since the eggs themselves, as well as the adults and the chicks when they emerge, are all cryptically coloured, breeding is seldom noticed except by the most observant.

JARVIS.

58. EDIBLE-NEST SWIFTLET
(Aerodramus fuciphagus)   (5"/13cm)

Swiftlets can be seen overhead at almost any time, anywhere on the island. One has to learn to watch out for their small size and rather stiff-winged flight. These birds are often erroneously referred to as swallows and are probably our most common aerial feeder. There are several colonies in different locations on the island, all in either complete or semi-darkness. They probably have acute vision which enables them to navigate in dim light, but their most powerful talent is their ability to echolocate. They are able to produce a series of audible clicks (up to 20 times per second), and by detecting the echo they are able to navigate in complete darkness. Although this system is very similar in principal to that used by bats, the sound is of a much lower frequency and is therefore audible to the human ear. The lower frequency also means that it is not sufficiently sensitive to allow them to catch their aerial insect prey with it. Hence they must feed in the daylight as other aerial feeders. The name of this species originates from the use of the nest in Chinese cuisine. A popular myth has it that the nest is made from regurgitated seaweed and is full of sea-borne nutrients. In reality it is constructed entirely from saliva produced by special glands below the tongue which swell during the breeding season. When hardened the saliva, or nest cement as it is known, dries to an opaque white colour. The nests are collected and boiled with a mixture of herbs and spices to form bird's nest soup, a great delicacy which is reputed to be good for a variety of ills. Chemical analysis of the material has shown it to be a muco-protein almost devoid of nutritive value. Great harm can be done to colonies by over-cropping and the removal of nests which contain eggs or nestlings. It takes almost four months for them to build a nest and raise two chicks. Successful colony management must allow for this.

59. BLACK-NEST SWIFTLET *(Aerodramus maximus)* (5.5"/14cm)

Almost identical in appearance and habits to the preceding species. It is slightly larger when seen alongside the Edible-nest Swiftlet and does not have the paler rump patch, although this is not a good field character and they are difficult to tell apart away from the nest. At the nest they are easily separated by the structure. As the name implies, this species has a nest which is very much darker, due to the presence of a large number of feathers. These feathers come from the birds' own plumage and are mixed in with saliva as it is applied to the nest. This may result in a more secure nest environment since they lay only a single large egg, as opposed to the two smaller ones of the Edible-nest bird. There is still sufficient saliva in the nest for it to be used for culinary purposes, but the extensive cleaning that they require makes the raw item less valuable. Colonies of this species in Singapore seem fairly secure for this reason, whereas those of the previous species are in great danger of being totally destroyed by poaching of the nests. Like other swiftlets they may be seen in dense flocks if an insect swarm is discovered, particularly when swept in front of a storm.

60

60. ASIAN PALM SWIFT *(Cypsiurus balasiensis)* (5"/13cm)

A delightful member of the swift family which gets its name from the habit of nesting in palm trees, where it forms loose colonies. It selects the broad-leaved type known as "fan palms", and seems especially fond of the genus *Livistona*. The nest is a small bracket of feathery seeds, often those of kapok. These are glued together with saliva and stuck onto the upper surface of the older leaves which hang down vertically from the crown of the palm. It is our smallest swift, with very pointed wings and a long forked tail which is often held nearly closed in flight. There is a small colony of them in the *Livistona* palms in Palm Valley in the Botanic Gardens; they roost in the same trees out of the breeding season and fly rapidly round them, giving their cheerful throaty warble, in the late evening.

61. HOUSE SWIFT
(Apus affinis) (6"/15cm)

The larger size and conspicuous white rump and throat patch of this bird readily distinguish it from the smaller swiftlets. Bucknill and Chasen described it as abundant in Singapore, but this is no longer the case. This is rather strange because it usually thrives in towns and cities; the whickering call of this species, as it performs its evening display flights before roosting, is a conspicuous feature of most Malaysian towns.

It builds a large untidy nest of feathers, straw, papers etc., glued together with saliva, under the eaves of houses and over five-foot ways. These nests do create a mess but they are usually tolerated since they are supposed to bring good fortune to the occupants. Although they used to nest in the city area it would seem that they have not done so for a good many years: evidence of old nesting can usually be seen ingrained in the paintwork of the older buildings. I know of only two or three places where these birds breed in any number.

Many of the birds which can be easily seen feeding over Singapore must nest either in Johore or on the offshore islands. Being one of the larger swifts they can fly very fast. Because they can move quickly from one insect swarm to another they can feed at great heights (about 200 m over the forest) where insects are rather scarce. Like most aerial feeders flying ants form a large part of the diet, and House Swifts seem particularly attracted to the larger types.

During the breeding season they switch from feeding high over forest to feeding at lower elevations over open country. This switch presumably keeps them closer to their nesting sites, which are not available in forest.

In the evening they can be easily viewed as they come down to drink at lakes and rivers.

JARVIS

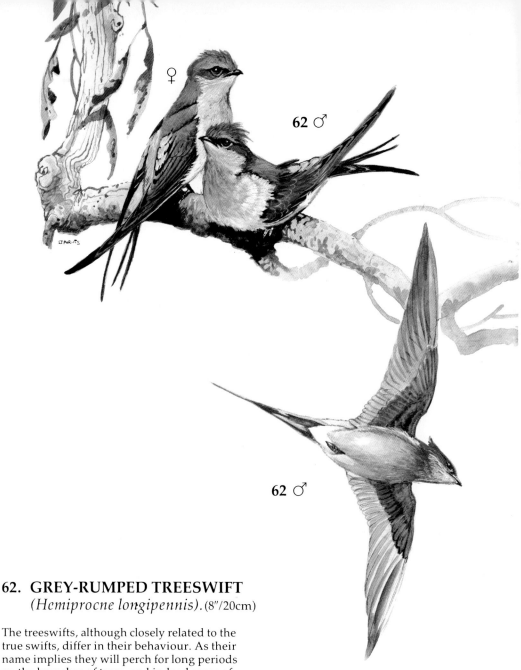

62 ♂

62 ♂

62. GREY-RUMPED TREESWIFT
(Hemiprocne longipennis). (8"/20cm)

The treeswifts, although closely related to the true swifts, differ in their behaviour. As their name implies they will perch for long periods on the branches of trees, and indeed some of them are more like flycatchers in their hunting behaviour. The Grey-rumped Treeswift appears dull in flight, but is well worth a good look in reasonable lighting. In flight they are rather reminiscent of Barn Swallows, but with stiffer wingbeats and a long forked tail which is often held closed. They tend to feed at a lower height than the true swifts, often in small loose flocks, and are quite vocal. The call is a shrill "cheerpit-cheerpit-cheerpitpit". In Singapore they seem to thrive quite well and are found in parks, mature gardens and in the rural areas, as well as the forest. They seem more common here than in similar habitats in Malaysia. The nest is a tiny cup of feathers and flakes of bark held together by saliva, fixed on the upper surface of a high branch. They lay only one egg and the whole assembly is totally hidden by the bird's body when incubating.

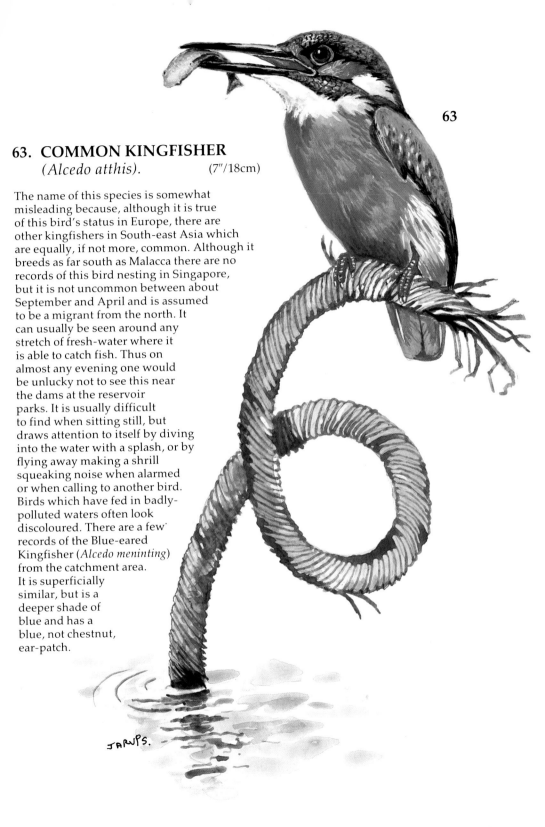

63. COMMON KINGFISHER
(*Alcedo atthis*). (7"/18cm)

The name of this species is somewhat
misleading because, although it is true
of this bird's status in Europe, there are
other kingfishers in South-east Asia which
are equally, if not more, common. Although it
breeds as far south as Malacca there are no
records of this bird nesting in Singapore,
but it is not uncommon between about
September and April and is assumed
to be a migrant from the north. It
can usually be seen around any
stretch of fresh-water where it
is able to catch fish. Thus on
almost any evening one would
be unlucky not to see this near
the dams at the reservoir
parks. It is usually difficult
to find when sitting still, but
draws attention to itself by diving
into the water with a splash, or by
flying away making a shrill
squeaking noise when alarmed
or when calling to another bird.
Birds which have fed in badly-
polluted waters often look
discoloured. There are a few
records of the Blue-eared
Kingfisher (*Alcedo meninting*)
from the catchment area.
It is superficially
similar, but is a
deeper shade of
blue and has a
blue, not chestnut,
ear-patch.

JARUPS.

64. WHITE-THROATED KINGFISHER *(Halcyon smyrnensis)* (11"/28cm)

This bird is not as common in Singapore as it is in the inland areas of the Malay Peninsula. It is one of the many representatives of this family which seldom eat fish. Although it is often seen near water it is more likely to be catching frogs or lizards in this situation. It is equally likely to be seen in trees far from water, diving to the ground for insects or small vertebrates. It has an enormous bright red beak, although not quite as large as that of the Stork-billed Kingfisher (which is a rarer, usually coastal, bird in Singapore), and unlike the next two species it has no white collar. The call is a harsh shrilling, "kee-ee-ee-ee" often uttered in flight. It also has a more mournful "yakking" call, faster and of a higher pitch than, but easily confused with, that of the Collared Kingfisher.

When it first alights on a new perch it will often bob its head and give a very high "chit" call. It seems to be very common around the perimeter of Changi Airport, where I once counted 17 birds spaced almost equally every 500m along the perimeter fence, although elsewhere in Singapore it is less common than the Collared Kingfisher. It makes its nest at the end of a fairly long burrow dug into a vertical, or very steep, bank. Whilst the excavation is underway the pair are very vocal, calling and displaying to each other continuously. In flight it has a white patch at the base of the primaries, very similar to that of the mynas. However the bright blue colouration prevents confusion with anything other than the Black-capped Kingfisher (see under that species).

65. COLLARED KINGFISHER *(Halcyon chloris)* (9.5"/24cm)

This is our most common kingfisher. It has its origins in coastal regions and mangroves, but as one proceeds south down the Malay Peninsula it occurs increasingly often inland, until arriving at Singapore it can be seen all over the island. However it still is more common around the coast, especially the muddy areas. It seems more aggressive than the White-throated Kingfisher and studies in Kuala Lumpur have shown it to be competitively superior to that bird. The White-throated certainly seems less common in Singapore than in former times and the spread of the Collared may account for this. It can also be seen interacting aggressively with the mynas, and will dive noisily on any flocks which are feeding within its territory in the breeding season. The mynas take fright at this and fly off quickly, screeching their alarm calls. The Collared will nest in holes in trees, in arboreal ant or termite nests (when still holding their original owners), and occasionally holes in a bank. When a pair are

seen together one always looks slightly more green than the other and this is the female; the male is bluer, especially on the primaries. But there is considerable variation in the plumage of each and this is not a reliable character for isolated individuals. The call is of a deeper tone than the White-throated and more of a coarse laugh, from which the Malay name *"pekak"* originates. Chasen has aptly described the call as a series of coarse "chacks" with a downward inflection, the first two of which are later repeated: 1-2-3-4-5, 1-2, 1-2, 1-2. They take a wide variety of food from fish, crabs and prawns (from which the other Malay name of *"rajah udang"* stems), to insects, frogs and lizards. They can be seen at their best on some of the offshore islands, especially the rocky ones such as St. John's or Sentosa. At low tide several can be seen dotted along the coast sitting on any suitable projection such as bush, rock or large piece of flotsam, from where they will dive down on to any foreshore animal exposed by the receding water.

66. BLACK-CAPPED KINGFISHER *(Halcyon pileata)* (12"/30cm)

Rather similar to the White-throated Kingfisher but can be told by the combination of a white collar and black cap. It sems to prefer to be around water slightly more than the White-breasted but is also happy in the middle of a dry park. It may be met with almost anywhere on the island but it is rather more shy than the other large kingfishers and therefore harder to see. A winter visitor to

Singapore from its breeding grounds in Burma and China, it seems to be able to fit in alongside our other kingfishers when it arrives. The call is very similar to that of the White-throated but mostly it is a rather silent bird. On the wing it has a conspicuous white patch just like that of the White-throated; look out for the black (not brown) wing coverts, black (not brown) cap, and white collar.

64

65

66

67. BLUE-TAILED BEE-EATER *(Merops philippinus)* (12"/30cm)

This bird is a winter visitor to Singapore in quite large numbers. Our bee-eaters complement each other because, as this species arrives, the Blue-throated, which breeds here, moves out and undergoes a seemingly pointless migration into Indonesia. At a distance the two look fairly similar, especially in flight, the Blue-tailed being identified by its pale throat. Immatures often lack the green cap and instead have a beige head, so a good look is required, especially at migration times when both may be present in fair numbers. It feeds in the open country and forest edge where it catches insects on the wing, usually returning to a perch to swallow them. They will roost communally and these roosts can sometimes reach huge proportions. I have twice seen roosts which numbered many hundreds of birds, once around the administrative buildings of the Institute of Education on Bukit Timah Road, and once in the form of a massive flock circling at dusk over the Serangoon estuary. They have also been found roosting in mangroves in Singapore.

67 imm.   ad.

106

68. BLUE-THROATED BEE-EATER *(Merops viridis)* (11″/28cm)

As stated left, this is superficially similar to the Blue-tailed. Young birds can be distinguished by their green cap instead of a chestnut one. They breed on the island but only in small numbers and their breeding colonies are not as easily found as one might expect. A large proportion of the population departs in late August and September for Indonesia, the few which remain (or perhaps they are arrivals from the north?) are found mainly in the forest areas, their place in the open country being taken by the Blue-tailed Bee-eater. Using the beak and feet a nest hole is dug in the ground. It is often built into a slight incline, but also on flat lawns and enters the ground at a shallow angle running down for three or four feet with a nest chamber at the end. It is usually found in sandy soil and this presumably is how they prevent the nest from becoming waterlogged. They will take a variety of bees and wasps, and are also fond of butterflies and dragonflies. Insects are snapped up (audibly!) in the air and then often beaten on a perch before swallowing; this latter action disarming the sting of the hymenoptera. The only place I have seen it breeding is near one of the quarries at Bukit Timah. It makes a pleasant sound upon which the Malay name *"berek-berek"* is based.

imm.

68 ad.

JARVIS.

69. DOLLARBIRD *(Eurystomus orientalis)* (12″/30cm)

On present evidence this bird is listed as a common winter visitor. It certainly is common in open country areas from October through to April, and I have very few records of it between the middle of May and the middle of August. It has been recorded breeding here in the past, with a different sub-species arriving in the northern winter. It is possible that a few pairs remain to breed but have yet to be discovered. A striking bird, its name originates from the bluish-white "dollar" seen on each wing in flight. But the red bill and feet are equally striking characteristics. It is a real aerial acrobat in display and will wheel and swoop in an impressive manner, from whence originates the alternative name of Broadbilled Roller. In flight it seems to have very long and flexible wings. It spends the hot part of the day sitting very still, often on the top of dead coconut trees, in which they are reported to breed. But it will also use any other high perch from which to make sorties at passing insects which are caught on the wing. It has a harsh, rasping call made up of a series of "chacks".

69

71

108

70. RED-CROWNED BARBET *(Megalaima rafflesii)*   (10"/25cm)

It is rather surprising that we now have only one of the forest barbets surviving in Singapore; however the Red-crowned Barbet does have a reputation for hanging on in disturbed habitats. The fact that it is now our sole representative of this group makes identification a lot easier. It is not terribly common and like most barbets tends to be heard more than seen. The call starts with a rather hesitant "poop-poop" followed by 10-15 steady "poops" at the rate of about three per second, all on one note. For such a large bird the call is surprisingly soft and it is well worth looking carefully up in the canopy in the direction from which it comes. Anyone familiar with other forest barbets in this region will know that several of them can give very powerful calls audible at a long distance, but not so this bird. As stated, it is inevitably seen up in the canopy, where it eats mostly fruit but will dig for grubs in the manner of the closely-related woodpeckers. I have seen birds excavating holes in dead trees where we assume they nest; an active nest found at Peirce Reservoir in 1978 seems to be the only record of breeding in Singapore or Malaysia.

71. COPPERSMITH BARBET *(Megalaima haemacephala)*   (6"/15cm)

This species underwent an invasion of the Malay Peninsula some years ago as successive deforested areas were joined up. In 1934 it was found in southern Perak, by 1939 it had reached Kuala Lumpur, by 1951 it was in Malacca, and in January 1957 it finally reached the Singapore Botanic Gardens. Since it can now be found on St. John's Island, two miles to the south, we must conclude the invasion is complete. It does not seem to have become particularly common here despite having had nearly 30 years in which to do so. It will undoubtedly benefit from the planting of ornamental fruit trees, especially figs, and this may account for an apparent increase in numbers over recent years. It can be found in many parts of the island, but is more common in the east from Sembawang to Changi, and is also a regular visitor to the fine fig trees in Fort Canning Park. It never penetrates into the forest. The name originates from the call which is a mellow, resonant, monotonous "poop" at the rate of slightly more than one per second. This is supposedly reminiscent of the noise of the coppersmith's hammer. Despite the bright colouration it is difficult to see, since it sits very still and the call is rather ventriloquial.

70

72. RUFOUS WOODPECKER *(Celeus brachyurus)* (10"/25cm)

This woodpecker is less common than the next species, with which it may be confused in poor light. It is, however, the only one in Singapore which is a rather even reddish-brown colour all over. The bill is a dark slate grey, and the male has a red cheek patch which is very difficult to see in all but the best light. The mantle is rufous but there are dark bars on the wings. It seems to be more common in the quieter rural areas, or around large suburban gardens. It can be seen in the forest but more often around the edge than in the centre. They build their nests in active arboreal ant or termite nests but they are very secretive. Nesting was observed by Ridley at the Botanic Gardens last century. It is said to eat a lot of ants, especially those from jackfruit trees; the feathers are often covered in sticky resin which may originate from the latex of these trees. The call is a series of descending "pui" notes.

73. BANDED WOODPECKER *(Picus miniaceus)* (10"/25cm)

This bird is most likely to be encountered in the forest of the Catchment Area. It must be observed carefully because it is very similar to the Crimson-winged Woodpecker which is reported from Singapore. The Banded Woodpecker is essentially a rather brown bird with bands on the plumage; however, the most conspicuous are those on the breast which, in the usual woodpecker pose, are almost impossible to see. The face and head of the male are entirely rufous-brown, whereas that of the female is brown spotted with white. The Crimson-winged Woodpecker is a predominantly green bird, with a large green mantle and green face with actually less crimson in the wing than the Banded! It also appears as a much brighter bird with a longer, more slender beak. The Banded Woodpecker is the most common of the larger woodpeckers in the forest and wooded areas, and is occasionally seen in the larger parks and gardens. Many textbooks also describe it as a bird of the mangroves but it is seldom encountered there in Singapore, presumably because the mangrove is now badly depleted and lacks tall trees. The most common call is a ringing "kwee", sometimes repeated intermittently, but always on the same note. At close quarters it makes a rather gentle "chewerk-chewerk-chewerk" on a rising scale.

74. LACED WOODPECKER *(Picus vittatus)* (12"/30cm)

This bird is the only all-green woodpecker to be found in Singapore. The male has a red crown and female black. It is fairly common in mangroves, especially on the landward edge. Also in old rubber or coconut estates near the coast. As in the peninsula this bird rarely penetrates far inland, although there is an increasing number of inland records and it is possible that this is another mangrove species colonising open country. The old name for this bird was Bamboo Green Woodpecker (now confusingly applied to a different species), and it does frequent larger bamboo clumps and will drum very loudly on the hollow stems. It can often be seen on the ground foraging at ant nests or termite mounds. The nest is usually excavated in old timber and is often within three or four feet of the ground. The call is a sharp "kyip" and it also has a chittering laugh on a descending scale.

75. COMMON GOLDENBACK *(Dinopium javanense)* (12"/30cm)

This bird is one of our more spectacular species. The male has a bright red crown whilst the female's is streaked black and white; in both it can be raised into a crest. In flight the red rump is conspicuous. It does not seem to be common in the forest or parks but is mainly in the rural areas, especially old coconut estates and mangrove fringes. They will occasionally visit gardens when they may sometimes be seen using a telegraph pole as a perch from which to call. They have been recorded feeding off the red *"kerengga"* ants amongst other insects; also the flesh and milk of coconuts, presumably using holes made by squirrels and bats to get into the latter. Their nest hole is usually fairly high off the ground and they favour dead coconut palms. I once saw one having a considerable argument with a Laced Woodpecker over the possession of a hole and it is possible that the two may compete for existing holes. The cry is a strident, clattering trill, descending in scale. Its flight call is a harsh "kee-kee-kee-keek" with pauses timed with the undulations of the flight.

73 ♂

♀

72 ♂

JARUPS.

111

76

JARVIS.

76. BROWN-CAPPED WOODPECKER *(Picoides moluccensis)* (5.25"/13cm)

This is the smallest of the woodpeckers (excluding the piculets of Malaysia) and is a very successful bird in Singapore. It is not found in the forest but occurs in every other habitat, including trees lining busy main roads. Originating from the mangroves, where it is still found in its greatest density, it is the classic example of an open country invader. Usually seen in pairs, although what I assume are family parties of four or five may sometimes be seen. They are always very active, concentrating their main feeding efforts on the smaller branches of trees in the mid-canopy. They are not very strong and nest

holes are usually excavated in the softer rotten wood such as dead branches and the old piles of jetties and piers near mangroves. When incubating they will often sit very still at the entrance hole with the beak protruding. Their presence is often betrayed by a rather cheerful little trill. The male has a red streak behind the eye, but in practice this seems to be limited to a single feather and is virtually impossible to see in the field. It is likely that many of the old records in Singapore of the very similar Grey-capped Woodpecker were in fact mis-identifications of this species, as there is no evidence of its presence on the island today.

75 ♂

75 ♀

74 ♀

74 ♂

JARVIS.

113

imm.

77 ad.

78

JARVIS.

77. BARN SWALLOW *(Hirundo rustica)* (6"/15cm)

This amazing little bird has an almost world-wide distribution, breeding throughout North America, and from Europe eastwards to China. In the winter there is a massive migration southwards with birds moving into South America, Africa, India and South-east Asia. An intensive ringing study in Malaysia showed that all of the birds in our area originate from eastern Asia. They can be seen in almost every month of the year but are very scarce in June. There is no evidence that any individuals remain here throughout the year but there is considerable overlap in the departure and arrival dates of different populations. Whilst in their southern quarters the birds undergo a moult which means they lose their distinctive tail streamers for a while. Also a large proportion of the winter population consists of juveniles which have a duller plumage, and a less distinct breast band. For these reasons they may be easily confused with the resident Pacific Swallow, the breast band and whiter underparts being the easiest characteristics to spot in flight. They form large communal roosts at night; in Malaysia they usually choose the service wires of the smaller towns, but in Singapore they have caused problems by roosting on oil installations and prefabricated open buildings. One roost which is easily seen is on the valve house at Seletar dam.

78. PACIFIC SWALLOW
(Hirundo tahitica) (5.5"/14cm)

Superficially very similar to the preceding species, but in all plumages it lacks the long tail streamers and never has a breast band. The underside is buffy-grey streaked with dark brown, giving it a rather dull appearance. It has more red on the forehead and throat than its temperate relative. They are usually found near water, whether it be the sea or rivers or canals, and they inevitably build their nests on man-made structures such as bridges or jetties which overhang water. This preference makes it mainly a coastal bird in Singapore, although the larger inland canals and reservoir dams will attract them. The nest is the usual swallow cup made from little globules of dried mud. Near the nest they tend to be easily alarmed and will fly off with a high-pitched "tweeet" at human approach. The song is a rather subdued but cheerful little twittering. In suitable locations they will form large breeding colonies. Outside the breeding season they will join the night-time roosts of the Barn Swallow.

115

14/6/99

79 ♂

♀

80 ♂

♀

JARVIS.

79. PIED TRILLER
(Lalage nigra)   (7"/18cm)

Although fairly common this bird often passes
unnoticed because of its rather shy, skulking
behaviour. The male is distinctive in that it has
a very pied appearance whereas the female has
rather more grey to it and is barred underneath
(this latter making it reminiscent of a
cuckoo). They also bear a similarity to
the next species. It looks an elongated
bird for its size, and carries the body
rather horizontally. It is not uncommon
in open country and gardens but is
most common in and around mangrove,
never in the forest. Frequenting the
middle and upper storey of trees, they
move with rather delibrate actions,
twisting the head around in their search
for insects. Usually seen in pairs or small
(four to five), family (?) parties. The name
triller is rather misleading because the call
is a rather nasal "chack-chack-chack-chack-
chack" on a descending scale. There are some
suggestions that they may undergo local
migrations but this has yet to be confirmed.
Pied Trillers have been seen feeding what are
thought to have been young Banded Bay
Cuckoos. Identification of these young cuckoos
is difficult and further observations on
fostering by this species are required. Older
texts refer to it as spending half its time feeding
on the ground, an activity I rarely seem to see.

80. ASHY MINIVET *(Pericrocotus divaricatus)* (8"/20cm)

In appearance this winter visitor is very similar to the Pied Triller. However it has a much more upright stance, a white forehead and not such a distinctive eyebrow. It has a wing bar visible from below in flight, but appearing as a row of white dots on the upper wing and only visible when the wing is spread. The female lacks the black on the head and is generally a paler bird. It is usually seen in tall coastal trees and often occurs in flocks of up to 50 individuals. These are noisy and fly in a rather bouncy manner, usually with the accompaniment of lots of noisy twittering. They are not particularly common but are met with spasmodically during the winter months. It arrives somewhat later than many other winter visitors, usually not appearing until November; it leaves again in early April.

81. COMMON IORA *(Aegithina tiphia)* (6"/15cm)

One of the more common birds of parks, gardens, mangrove and open country, it appears generally yellow-green with two white wing bars. In breeding plumage the male can assume a beautiful canary yellow colour. The crown and back of the male varies from green to black and in Singapore there seems to be a higher proportion of the dark birds than elsewhere. Such can be the contrast with the yellow colour that the bird almost seems to have a dark ruff of feathers on the head. The rump can occasionally appear white because they have long, pale flank feathers which often overlap it. They hunt for insects at a fairly high level in the tree canopy, and are said to be fond of mistletoe berries. They possess a host of calls which are variants of a clear whistled "pui-puoor-pui", sometimes down the scale, sometimes wavering up and down. A most characteristic call is one which involves a long, drawn out, rather tremulous note switching rapidly to a much shorter one almost an octave lower, the whole having a most mournful air to it — "wheeeeee-tiu" repeated several times.

82. YELLOW-VENTED BULBUL (*Pycnonotus goiavier*) (8"/20cm)

This is probably the most numerous bird in Singapore, being found in every habitat with the exception of the dense forest. Although a rather dull bird, the sulphur yellow undertail coverts do provide a splash of colour. The most obvious character is probably the black line which encloses the eye and runs forward to the beak, coupled with a white eyebrow and a dark brown crown which imparts a very striped appearance to the head. It has a cheerful, rich bubbling song which is the main sound of almost all parks and gardens at dawn and dusk. A small crest on the crown is often raised and lowered whilst singing. Out of the breeding season they will form small communal roosts, usually in very dense bushes or trees, the Bunga Tanjong (*Mimusops elengi*) being a favourite. Part of their success is attributable to their very wide choice of food items, ranging from a variety of fruits, through insects to scavenging on scraps of food. They may also be seen in the evening catching flying termites, along with a variety of aerial feeders. They are so used to human company that it is not unusual to find their deep, cup-shaped nests in ornamental pot plants on balconies and verandas. Long-term netting and ringing of these birds on one site in Malaysia yielded high catches but a very low re-trap rate (less than seven percent). This suggests that the birds are nomadic. It is interesting to think that our supposed "resident" garden pairs may actually be several different individuals changing all the time as the year progresses.

83. OLIVE-WINGED BULBUL (*Pycnonotus plumosus*) (8"/20cm)

In Singapore this bird complements almost exactly the Yellow-vented Bulbul: any habitat not invaded by the latter is the haunt of this species. Thus it is found mainly in the forests of the Nature Reserve and Catchment Area, to a lesser extent in the mangroves and rather rarely in the more heavily wooded rural areas. It is a heavier bird, all olive-green, and the patch on the wing which gives rise to the name is obvious only in good light. It has a darkish eyebrow which tends to give it the appearance of a scowl. It has become one of the most common birds in the forests, perhaps as a result of the lack of many other forest bulbuls since it seems much more common in Singapore than elsewhere. Like its close relative it will eat both fruit and insects. The song is somewhat reminiscent of the Yellow-vented Bulbul in tone, but is rather clipped and more sharply phrased, but still melodious.

84. CREAM-VENTED BULBUL (*Pycnonotus simplex*) (7"/18cm)

This is the smallest of the Singapore bulbuls. Entirely brown with a pale buff throat and belly. The most distinctive features are the white iris and cream undertail coverts. Found only in the forested areas it is less common than the Olive-winged Bulbul. It also seems to keep mostly to the taller, older stands of trees as opposed to the scrubby secondary growth. It seems to eat mostly fruit but in fact its habit have been little studied. The call is a hysterical, rapidly repeated "chirriup". Juvenile birds have a yellowish-orange iris, leading to confusion with the Red-eyed Bulbul (*P. brunneus*) which is uncommon in Singapore. The Red-eyed has a brick-red iris and a much darker, olive-brown, throat and belly than the Cream-vented.

84

JARVIS.

82

83

JARVIS.

85. BLACK DRONGO (*Dicrurus macrocercus*) (11″/28cm)

A few years ago this species seemingly underwent an extension of its range. Resident in the more northern parts of South-east Asia, it was known to winter in southern Thailand and northern Malaysia. It was found in Selangor and Malacca in 1976–1977 and the first record from Singapore was in 1978–1979. It now occurs regularly in small numbers each winter, although all these observations may only reflect increase in observer competence. It has the appearance of a small, black crow, with a deeply forked tail and upright stance. The plumage does not have a glossy sheen like other drongos, and the juveniles have the breast flecked with white. They are usually found in open country, preferably near long grass, where they choose an exposed perch from which to pursue passing insects. Thus a favourite place tends to be the telecommunications towers at Upper Jurong Road where they perch on the supporting guy wires. I have also seen them on older reclaimed land which has become covered in weeds, sitting on the tops of bushes or wooden stakes.

JARVIS.

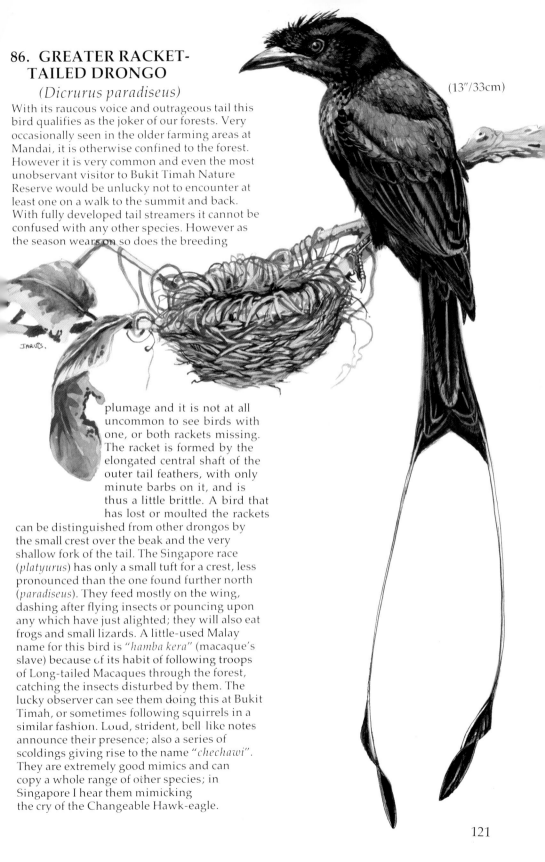

86. GREATER RACKET-TAILED DRONGO
(Dicrurus paradiseus)

(13"/33cm)

With its raucous voice and outrageous tail this bird qualifies as the joker of our forests. Very occasionally seen in the older farming areas at Mandai, it is otherwise confined to the forest. However it is very common and even the most unobservant visitor to Bukit Timah Nature Reserve would be unlucky not to encounter at least one on a walk to the summit and back. With fully developed tail streamers it cannot be confused with any other species. However as the season wears on so does the breeding plumage and it is not at all uncommon to see birds with one, or both rackets missing. The racket is formed by the elongated central shaft of the outer tail feathers, with only minute barbs on it, and is thus a little brittle. A bird that has lost or moulted the rackets can be distinguished from other drongos by the small crest over the beak and the very shallow fork of the tail. The Singapore race (*platyurus*) has only a small tuft for a crest, less pronounced than the one found further north (*paradiseus*). They feed mostly on the wing, dashing after flying insects or pouncing upon any which have just alighted; they will also eat frogs and small lizards. A little-used Malay name for this bird is *"hamba kera"* (macaque's slave) because of its habit of following troops of Long-tailed Macaques through the forest, catching the insects disturbed by them. The lucky observer can see them doing this at Bukit Timah, or sometimes following squirrels in a similar fashion. Loud, strident, bell-like notes announce their presence; also a series of scoldings giving rise to the name *"chechawi"*. They are extremely good mimics and can copy a whole range of other species; in Singapore I hear them mimicking the cry of the Changeable Hawk-eagle.

JARVIS.

87 ♀

♂

imm.

JARUPS.

87. BLACK-NAPED ORIOLE *(Oriolus chinensis)* (10.5″/27cm)

A very distinctive bird of parks, gardens and open areas. The large size and bright yellow colouration of the adults prevents confusion with any other species. The name comes from the black band which stretches around the back of the neck. The mantle of the female is more green than that of the male, whilst the juveniles are heavily streaked on the breast and green on the back. It has a range of very clear flute-like whistles, the most conspicuous of which is "tooo-diddlyoo". It also makes several harsh rasping noises which sound as though it may be annoyed, although the source of the problem is never seen. Two races of this bird are found in the region but they are virtually indistinguishable in the field. The northern race breeds in Indo-china and migrates into the north of the Malay peninsula. The resident breeding population, which are the birds seen in Singapore, are the results of an invasion from Indonesia in the early 1930's. This invasion may have been helped by the escape of caged birds. It is now a well established species in Singapore and has been so since at least 1938. It seems to have a varied diet: it can usually be seen feeding off ripe figs and other fruits and I have seen it several times with a large Praying Mantis in its beak. It is sometimes observed being chased by other birds in the breeding season and I suspect that it may rob the nests of smaller birds. The nest has been recorded as being placed high up in the fork of a tree, the two eggs being bluish-white with brown spots.

88. ASIAN FAIRY-BLUEBIRD *(Irena puella)* (10″/25cm)

One of the most spectacular birds in Singapore, but unfortunately not easy to see since it is a canopy-feeding frugivore which is confined to the forest area. Thus the all-too-familiar view is of a black silhouette against the bright sky. They are not uncommon, however, and patient watching from the steep road up Bukit Timah Hill can reveal one in the canopy of the trees below. They are very often seen in pairs but whether they mate for life is unknown. The call is a series of very clear whistles; one is a drawn out "whee-eet" on a rising scale, often preceded by several shorter notes on a descending scale viz: "whip-whip-whip-whip-whip-whip-whip, whee-eet".

88 ♂

89. LARGE-BILLED CROW
(*Corvus macrorhynchos*) (20"/51cm)

Larger than the House Crow, this bird lacks the grey collar, having a glossy black appearance all over. The name originates from the large powerful beak, much larger relative to the head than in the House Crow. It tends to be rather solitary, occuring most often in singles or pairs. It eats a variety of foodstuffs, but relies much less on man for its living than the House Crow, taking mostly natural food or offal. It may occasionally be seen in the town but is more often encountered in the rural areas, mangrove and coastal parks, and rarely near houses. Thus although it is branded a "crow", and as such a "pest", it in fact does little to cause humans any inconvenience. Only the farmers may have justifiable complaints because they will prey upon young chicks or ducklings and have even been known to attack weak or sickly piglets. It is said to occasionally build its nest alongside that of the White-bellied Sea Eagle. The call is a stentorial "caw" of a deeper pitch than the House Crow, and also a curious gurgling sound.

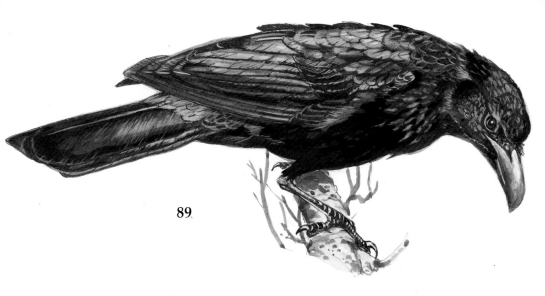

89.

JARVIS.

90. HOUSE CROW (*Corvus splendens*) (17"/43cm)

The ubiquitous urban commensal found in many countries throughout Asia. Originating from India and Sri Lanka, the Singapore (and Malaysian) population seems to have been introduced from the latter. Gibson-Hill (1949) makes reference to a failed attempt to introduce them before the war. However the present population became established at some point during the turbulent war years. It spread to every part of the island and, although no counts were ever made, the general opinion is that the population is now smaller than it was formerly. To what extent this is due to the shooting of it as a pest, or to improvements in environmental cleanliness, is unknown. The population density achieved on the offshore islands is far greater than that on the main island, possibly due to the relatively greater coastline, and also discarded food from picnickers, both of which afford more scavenging opportunities. It is so well adapted to living off man's waste that man-made objects are often incorporated into the nest. Many have been found which are constructed almost entirely out of stiff wire. It is primarily a scavenger and so is to be found around the coasts, river mouths and rubbish tips. Its guile at stealing food from man makes it infamous. It will also utilise the natural foods of fruiting roadside trees when these are available. They will form large communal roosts, although in Singapore these seem to be confined to offshore islands. There seems to be free interchange of birds with those in Johore. It is said locally that the ash of crow feathers mixed with coconut milk is a certain cure for baldness and premature greying hair; but this magic does not seem to have endangered its existence in Singapore in any way. Although the eggs and nestlings are probably at risk from snakes, the adults seem to have no real enemies. In India the Koel (a cuckoo — *Eudynamis scolopacea*) parasitises the nest of the House Crow, but it is only a non-breeding visitor to Singapore.

125

91. STRIPED TIT-BABBLER (*Macronous gularis*) (5.25"/13cm)

This is by far the most common of our babblers, being found throughout the forested areas where it is most common, but occasionally also on mangrove fringes and in more densely wooded rural areas. It usually occurs mid-way between the ground and the tree canopy, often foraging among lianes and climbers. It is a fairly dull yellow-brown, darker on the upper surface and with heavy streaks on the underside and head. It usually occurs in parties of between four and ten. We know that babblers elsewhere are often co-operative breeders, that is, they will assist in raising the offspring of close relatives. The fact that this species occurs in parties may mean that it does the same thing. The breeding habits of the forest babblers of South-east Asia have never undergone a detailed examination. This bird utters a monotonous "chonk", repeated ad nauseum throughout the day, it is often the only bird to be heard in the forest during the heat of the afternoon. It also has a series of scolding churrs, rather similar to those of the Chestnut-winged Babbler.

92. CHESTNUT-WINGED BABBLER
(Stachyris erythroptera) (5.5″/14cm)

Another shy babbler found only in the forest areas. It again inhabits low vegetation in the understorey and forest edge, and is often seen where there are ferns bordering on taller trees. It has a grey-blue head and deep chestnut wings. The *Stachyris* babblers have blue skin on the head which in this species may be seen in the form of a patch around the eye and in two patches either side of the throat when the latter is inflated for calling. It is rather more confiding than the Short-tailed Babbler and will often approach close if one stands very still. The song is a stuttered series of "poops" which slide down to a lower pitch half-way through, the whole lasting only about two seconds. It also makes a series of scolding "churrs" and I am not sure whether these are part of a duet, a contact call, or an alarm call. The nest has been described as a ball of dried leaves within three metres of the ground.

JARVIS.

93. SHORT-TAILED BABBLER (Trichastoma malaccense) (5.5″/14cm)

This babbler is found only in the Nature Reserve and catchment area. It is rather wary, and may easily be overlooked, although the calls can be heard often enough. It is usually seen on, or very close to, the forest floor, habits for which the short tail is appropriate. Good views are not easily obtained and the most conspicuous features for identification are the black "moustache", grey cheeks and orange-buff underparts. It seems to have suffered through forest disturbance since it is not as common in Singapore as in secondary forest in Malaysia. The two most frequently heard calls are: a) six to seven wavering notes descending the scale often followed immediately by b) four sharply whistled "teuu" notes all on the same pitch. They are easy to mimic and the bird will readily investigate a good imitation.

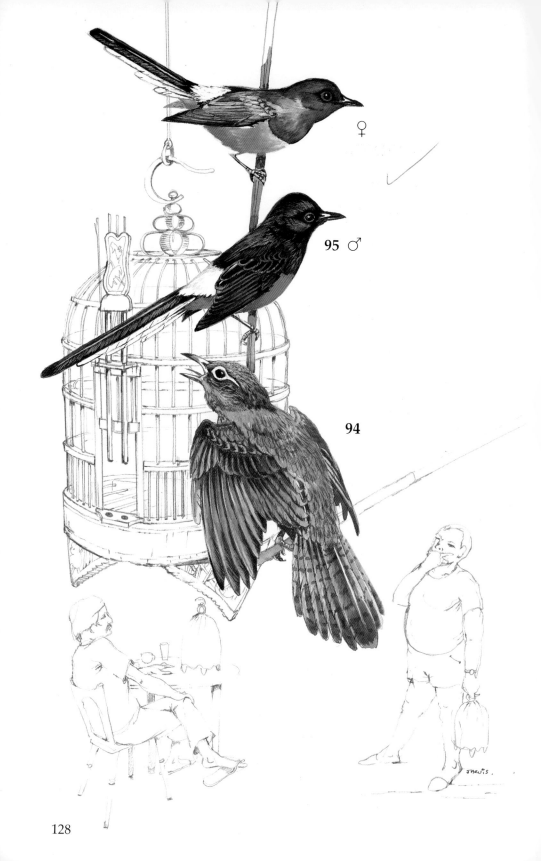

♀

95 ♂

94

JARVIS.

128

94. HWAMEI (*Garrulax canorus*)   (10"/25cm)

This is not a native species in Singapore but one which originates from further north in Indo-china and southern China. It is valued as a cage bird for its rather harsh and persistent song which is a series of hard "teu" notes all on the same pitch. It is entered into singing contests where large sums of money may be at stake. Sufficient numbers have now escaped, or been deliberately released, that they are well established in Singapore and presumed to be breeding, although I do not know of any records as yet. I have only once seen it on the edge of the forest areas and it would appear to prefer more open country. They may be seen most commonly in parks and gardens where they will dive down from bushes to take insects from the ground. In this respect they resemble our hard-pressed Magpie Robin in habits, and one hopes that they are not in competition with the attractive native species.

95. WHITE-RUMPED SHAMA (*Copsychus malabaricus*)   (11"/28cm)

This is the forest equivalent of the Magpie Robin, to which it is closely related. Never found away from forested areas, it is a rather shy skulking bird even in the gloom of the understorey which it frequents. The song is very spectacular, consisting of a series of deep warblings of a rather fruity quality. It is the song, and its ability to mimic other species, which has been its downfall. For, like the Magpie Robin, there are now many more shamas in cages in coffee shops around Singapore than one could ever find in the forest. In fact I have only encountered this bird in the wild in Singapore on three occasions, and each of these I have assumed to be lucky escapees, or cast-offs which failed their owner in the last "singing" contest, and which have found their way back to the forest habitat. None of these was seen on a second occasion and I am fairly confident that they will now be ensconsed in a bamboo prison entertaining a new captor. As long as this situation prevails I can see no future in Singapore for any wild members of this species. A concerted captive breeding programme by the cage-bird societies and dealers could ensure an adequate supply for hobbyists and allow for the re-introduction of the birds to the wild.

96. MAGPIE ROBIN (*Copsychus saularis*)   (8.5"/22cm)

Also known as the Straits Robin, *Murai* or just plain Magpie. Writing in 1927, Buknill and Chasen described this as "... so common in Singapore that it needs no mention ... In the gardens it is one of the most familiar of birds." These observations still apply to the peninsula, where it is a common sight, with most mature gardens having its resident pair. In Singapore the situation is very different and I only know of less than 20 wild individuals on the whole island. The cause of its downfall appears to be habitat disturbance coupled with widescale intensive trapping for the cage bird trade. During the breeding season males are very aggressive and easily netted with the aid of a decoy male. They are prized as "singing" birds and may be found in cages everywhere on the island. Most pet shops or bird dealers will have large cages full of bedraggled specimens with damaged wings and pulled tail feathers, due to the ill-treatment they receive when imported into Singapore. This is a tragedy because the adult birds have a fine, deep, glossy plumage and a song which is a strong pure whistle, very sweet and melodious. The sorry specimens we see caged bear hardly any resemblance to their wild relatives. Attempts are currently underway to re-introduce this species to protected areas. Ringed birds are breeding successfully and if their offspring can be properly protected there is a chance that their status may be recovered.

JARVIS.

97. FLYEATER
(Gerygone sulphurea)   (3.5"/9cm)

This is perhaps one of the most widely
distributed of our birds inhabiting virgin
forests, mangroves, parks and gardens,
plantations and *kampongs*. There does not seem
to be a habitat that this little species has not
ventured into. It is easily overlooked, despite
being common, because it is one of the smallest
birds and coloured with subtle tones which
blend well with the vegetation. This, coupled
with inconspicuous habits, appears to have
been the cause of its omission from all the bird
lists of Singapore until recent times. As the
name suggests, it is an insectivorous species.
The nest is a pendant, similar in construction
to that of the Brown-throated Sunbird, being
made of cobwebs, fine fibres and lichens, with
a hole at the side for an entrance. The Malayan

Bronze Cuckoo is reported as parasitising this
species. The surest means of recording its
presence is to learn its thin, reedy whistle, like
someone whistling gently through their teeth,
the notes meandering up and down the scale.
The bird will turn its head from side to side
whilst singing, giving a ventriloquial effect
that makes the singer hard to locate.

98. GREAT REED-WARBLER *(Acrocephalus orientalis)* (7.5"/19cm)

A very large warbler with a darkish crown, buffy-white eyebrow and light underparts. Plumage-wise it has little else to distinguish it but always seems to have a rather stern countenance and an upright stance. It is rather a skulker, and if you focus attention on it it becomes even more so. It can usually be seen in marshy areas, either on passage or as a winter visitor. Thus the wetlands around Kranji dam are ideal, but it will also occur in scrubland, mangrove and occasionally parks and gardens; never forest. It makes a grating "kek" or "chak" call and has a characteristic deep song which can sometimes be heard in the spring before they depart: "karra-karra-kee-kaa-kaa-kaa" (King et al), usually sung whilst hidden.

131

99

99. ARCTIC WARBLER *(Phylloscopus borealis)* (5"/13cm)

Another species which is easily missed because of its canopy-feeding habits and dull colouration. It is, however, the most commonly seen of the leaf warblers and can be observed in almost any type of habitat in Singapore during the months that it is here. It occurs as a passage migrant and winter visitor and has a long stay, the latest departures being in June and the earliest arrivals in August. Of course we have no idea just how long any one individual will remain here. It is a rather dull green above, yellow-green below, with a conspicuous creamy-yellow eyebrow and a very faint wing bar which can sometimes appear double. It makes a characteristic "zit", and has a rattling song, quite often heard from March onwards, consisting of a series of rapid "chweet" notes strung together.

100. COMMON TAILORBIRD *(Orthotomus sutorius)* (4.75"/12cm)

Also known as the Long-tailed Tailorbird because of the extended central tail feathers of the male in breeding plumage. The tailorbirds can be very hard for the beginner to separate because they are rather similar and often skulk around in low vegetation. The Common Tailorbird has the least red on the head of any of them, and red thighs, although these are seldom seen. It is often mistakenly identified as the Dark-necked because the dark feather bases show through on the neck, especially when singing. But they show as dark streaks on the side of the neck, not a dark collar underneath the throat as in the other species. It is the tailorbird most likely to be encountered in parks, gardens and open country. Tailorbirds get their name from the method of constructing a nest. The edges of a large leaf, or perhaps two small ones, are pulled together and held there by plant fibres or spider webs sewn through holes made specially for this purpose. The ends of the fibres are then teased out into a ball (not knotted as some people claim) which locks them against the hole. The nest is then made in the pouch, formed of grass and other plant materials, often lined with kapok or other soft seeds. The most common type is made of only one leaf; in this case the pouch hangs underneath and the surface of the leaf forms a waterproof roof which is also ideally camouflaged. The song is a rather monotonous "chwee-o" repeated so quickly that at any distance it sounds just as one note, "chweep-chweep-chweep".

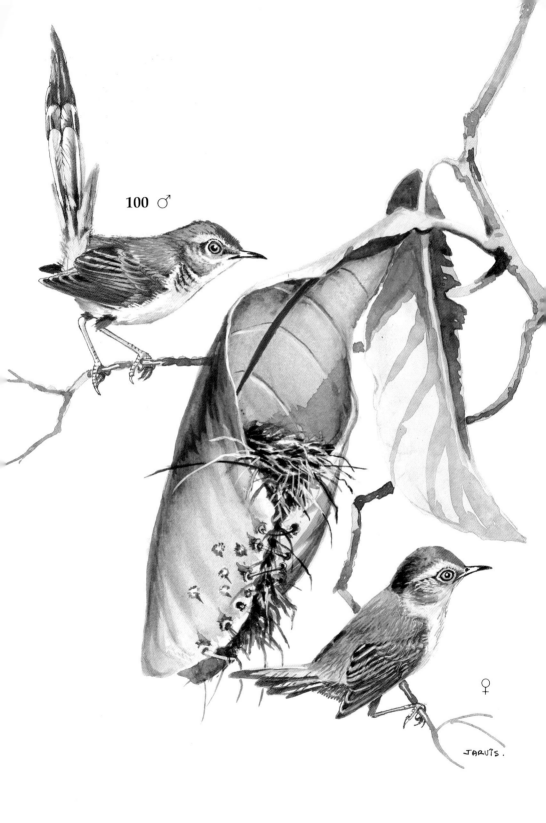

100 ♂

♀

JARUTS.

101. DARK-NECKED TAILORBIRD *(Orthotomus atrogularis)* (4.3"/11cm)

A bird predominantly of the forest and denser scrub. The male has an entirely red cap, a distinctive black collar and yellow undertail coverts. The female lacks the first two features and may be easily mistaken for the Common Tailorbird. The habits are much the same as the Common, it being confined to dense undergrowth, seldom venturing to any height in the tree canopy. It is rarely seen in parks and gardens, however, as the undergrowth is seldom thick enough, but it does get into the more densely wooded agricultural areas. It has several calls, all of them more shrill than the common; a disyllabic "koo-chit, koo-chit, koo-chit" and a monosyllabic "pree-pree-pree" are the two frequently heard, but it also has other reels and trills. As with all tailorbirds it will make a "zit-zit" call as it searches for insects.

102. RUFOUS-TAILED TAILORBIRD *(Orthotomus sericeus)* (4.5"/11cm)

This is perhaps the nicest looking of the four tailorbirds found in Singapore. It is more heavily built than the others, the entire cap the usual rufous colour, but this is contrasted by a rich creamy colour below the eye and over the throat, darkening a little on the breast and underparts; the upperparts are the same ash-grey as the Ashy. Like the rest of this group the short wings, designed to function in dense vegetation, result in a weak flight made with rather a flicking action. It is rather local in its distribution, occasionally in gardens but more often in scrub and edges of cultivation or mangrove, and never in the forest. Where it occurs it is fairly common, but there are seemingly large areas of suitable habitat where it is absent. The call is trisyllabic, rising on the middle note, "kuachi-kuachi-kuachi".

103. ASHY TAILORBIRD *(Orthotomus ruficeps)* (4.5"/11cm)

This tailorbird is very aptly named since the entire body is a dark ash-grey colour; the rufous of the cap extends below the eye to cover the entire face of both male and female. Although it will occasionally visit gardens and plantations these are usually near the coast, because this is predominantly a bird of the mangroves, where it is very common. Like the rest of the family it usually feeds very low down, although none of the Singapore mangroves are tall and therefore this observation may be misleading. The call is a ringing "wheeeee-chip, wheeeee-chip" and also "preee, preee, preee", rather like the Dark-necked in quality. On the offshore islands the Ashy Tailorbird seems to have spread all over the island and is not restricted to the coast.

Identifying Tailorbirds

	COMMON	DARK-NECKED	ASHY	RUFOUS-TAILED
HEAD	forehead red	entire crown red (m), forehead red (f)	face & forehead red	entire crown red
BACK	olive	olive	grey	grey
UNDER-PARTS	pale buff	pale buff with dark collar	grey	buffy-white with creamy throat and cheeks
OTHER	long tail (m) red thighs	yellow under-tail coverts	red thighs	red tail & thighs

101 ♂

♀

102

103

JARVIS.

135

104. YELLOW-BELLIED PRINIA
(Prinia flaviventris)   (5.5"/14cm)

A small resident warbler only found in areas
where there is a good stand of long grass. It is
often difficult to see because it stays within the
grass, hopping sideways up to the top of the
tall stalks to scan around or sing its cheerful
song, diving down into the stalks at the merest
hint of danger. It is very common in the long
grass of Kranji reservoir and also in old
coconut estates and abandoned land behind
the mangroves. It is easily identified by the
long tail, yellow belly, white throat and breast
and grey head; it has a bright red eye. Its food
consists entirely of insects. The nest is a grass
dome wrapped around several tall stalks and
made into a ball, the entrance being at the side.
It is usually about two feet off the ground, the
stalks keeping the nest from falling and
effectively disguising it. When alarmed this
bird will fly in a rather weak and top-heavy
manner, making a sharp clicking noise
apparently coming from the wings. The song is
a very distinctive and sudden "chip-
cheererere-up". It will also make a rather
nasal "waa" sound like a hungry kitten,
which seems to be an alarm call.

105. BROWN FLYCATCHER
(Muscicapa latirostris) (5.25"/13cm)

A rather dull little bird appearing greyish-
brown on the head and back, and pale buff
underneath. It has a pale ring around the eye
giving it a very wide-eyed appearance.
Flycatchers do just as the name says, catching
their food from insects which fly past. They
will fly up from their perch to snap at an
insect, often returning to the same
spot again. They may do this several
times before changing to a different
location to repeat the exercise. The Brown
Flycatcher will often be seen doing this
from an exposed branch. It is not resident, only
visiting Singapore during the northern winter
from September to April. It can be seen in
parks and gardens, mangrove and forest. Birds
seen in the forest are worth a close look
since we also get the Dark-sided
Flycatcher there; this has darker underparts
with a pale streak down the centre of
the breast and belly. Also, in the
mangroves beware of confusion with the
Mangrove Whistler. There is a rufous race
(*williamsoni*) resident in Malaysia, but only
recorded as a migrant in Singapore.

106. ZITTING CISTICOLA
(Cisticola juncidis)   (4.5"/11cm)

Another small warbler of
grassland areas, which can also
be extremely difficult to see.
It is a small, rather undistinguished brown streaked
bird with a rusty-buff rump.
It does not use very long grass
in the way the previous species
does but stays more around
shorter grass, again in search of
insects. But it builds its open cup
nest at the base of a tuft of long
grass which it will dive into
when danger threatens.
It has an interesting
display flight in which
it spirals very high in
the air with jerky wing-
beats and then hovers
there with tail spread, giving
a clockwork-sounding "tik, tik, tik"
almost continuously, before
diving headlong back into the
grass again. In some parts, and
formerly in this region, this bird is
known as the Fantail Warbler. It can be
seen at Kranji reservoir and around
the fringes of the golf courses.

106

105

107. PIED FANTAIL *(Rhipidura javanica)* (7"/18cm)

Fantails feed by carrying out a madcap chase through the vegetation, picking up insects anywhere they occur. All the while the long tail is constantly fanned open and then closed again. This action flashes the white feather tips and presumably disturbs insects, forcing them to reveal their presence and become potential prey items. It is more common in or near mangrove areas but, with the exception of the forest, can be seen in almost any habitat where the vegetation is dense. The nest is built at eye level, usually in a fork, and is a neat inverted cone of plant fibres plastered with spiders' webs, often with a delicate tail underneath. The Pied Fantail has a rather coarse, halting little song which is uttered whilst chasing insects — "chup-chup-chup-choowoot-cheweet-choowoot". This rather disorganised song, coupled with its madcap hunting method, has resulted in the Malay name *"murai gila"* — crazy thrush.

108

plexa

taivana

simillima

108

108. YELLOW WAGTAIL *(Motacilla flava)* (7"/18cm)

A common winter visitor which is seen most often on short turf where it picks insects off the grass whilst walking (not hopping) hurriedly along. It occasionally jumps upwards to catch insects in the air. It seems to prefer flooded areas and is often seen in flocks of a hundred or more birds around the edge of puddles on golf courses and playing fields. There are many races, or sub-species, of this bird found in different regions of the world and our birds show variation in plumage, especially in the colouration of the head which may vary from green to a bluish-grey. For the connoisseur, the races so far identified have been *simillima*

107

JARVIS.

(common, blue-headed type, with a white streak behind the eye), *taivana* (less common, green-headed with a yellow eye-stripe), and *plexa* (rather rare, dark-grey head with blackish ear-coverts). All are present in Singapore from September to May. The variations in head colour are best seen towards the end of this period, before their departure north. For many of the earlier months the plumage has a dull, olive-grey appearance. This makes them difficult to see on the ground but they can be detected by their sharp "tzweep" contact call. They seem to form communal roosts as I have seen a hundred or more in bushes at dusk.

109. RICHARD'S PIPIT (8"/20cm)
(*Anthus novaeseelandiae*)

A very common bird of short grassland, seen on golf courses, playing fields and the larger parks, usually singly or in pairs, never in flocks. It is essentially a bird of the ground where its long pink legs give it a characteristic bold, upright stance. The plumage is unremarkable, streaked brown with slightly heavier streaking on the breast, and a buff eyebrow. It will occasionally fly to a vantage point such as a post or small bush. When in flight the white outer tail feathers can be seen. On the ground it catches small insects by running forwards in short bursts. It has an undulating display flight when it glides downwards and flies up again giving a series of rattling "tchissip" calls. The nest is a shallow cup built on the ground in a tussock of long grass.

110. BROWN SHRIKE (*Lanius cristatus*) (7.7"/20cm)

Of the two shrikes which occur in Singapore as winter visitors this species is the one most often encountered in open country, parks and gardens. The adult birds have a conspicuous black mask; this is absent in the immature birds of which we see a large number. The latter may be identified by their dull plumage with much barring on the breast. It is a very noisy bird and seems to be one of the few species which defends a territory in its winter quarters. They do this with harsh grating, chattering calls. They feed on insects which are often taken from the ground, pounced upon from a high perch and the larger ones held with a foot whilst they are consumed. There are four separate races which have been recorded from Singapore but only two are really common — *superciliosus*, which has a chestnut head and back and passes through on migration south, and *confusus*, with an ash-brown head and back

111. TIGER SHRIKE (7.5"/19cm)
(*Lanius tigrinus*)

Although newly-arrived migrants do come down in open country this shrike is more likely to be met with in the forest. It is slightly smaller than the Brown Shrike but with a heavier bill (Thick-billed Shrike was the old name). The adults are easily told by their grey heads and rich chestnut plumage barred with black. Juveniles (which seem to form the majority of birds in Singapore) are difficult to tell from juveniles of the preceding species: they have a brown head and back, heavily barred with black, and the black patch over the ear tends to be barred. Shrikes are known to impale insects on thorns and store them as food "larders"; the Brown Shrike has been seen to do this but I do not know of any similar observations for the Tiger Shrike and presume it is either uncommon or a habit they do not adopt.

111 imm.

110 *superciliosus*

imm.

confusus

111 ♀

♂

112. HILL MYNA
(*Gracula religiosa*) (12"/30cm)

Although classified as a myna the habits and appearance of this bird are very different from any of the others found in Singapore. A small number thrive in the Botanic Gardens but it is most likely to be met with in the forest inhabiting the tree canopy, where it eats mainly fruit. It is often seen in pairs and like other mynas it may mate for life. It is very vocal and the main call is a ringing "tiong" which gives rise to its Malay name; it will also emit a whole series of most unusual grunts and groans. The calls are very often made from the top of a tall dead tree. Its vocal abilities have made it a popular cage bird since it can be taught to mimic the human voice, and large numbers are removed from the wild in Sumatra India and Burma to provide amusement in Singapore's coffee shops. The occasional records of this bird in suburban areas are assumed to originate from escapes of these caged birds. With its orange-red beak and yellow lappets of the skin on the head it cannot be confused with any other species.

113. PHILIPPINE GLOSSY STARLING (*Aplonis panayensis*) (8"/20cm)

A very familiar bird to all, although generally known by its Malay name of "*perling*". The adult birds are worth a long look in bright sunlight because their plumage can change from brilliant green through purple to black depending on how the sun strikes them; this display contrasts with the bright red eye. The juveniles are quite different, with a cream breast heavily streaked with black, and a dull green-grey back. They feed mainly on fruit and large numbers will congregate in trees such as figs and *tembusu* when in fruit. They will occasionally come to the ground for fallen fruits, especially below palm trees, but tend to move rather clumsily and look awkward. They have the social habits of the family and are mostly found in flocks. The flight is swift and direct and the flocks fairly compact. At night flocks will join together in large communal roosts. Before descending into their chosen trees they perform impressive aerial display flights, wheeling and twisting in large numbers over the roost site. It is thought that this behaviour is designed to advertise the roost, to attract as many birds as possible to it, but this is uncertain. They nest in a variety of holes, including those in trees as well as the eaves of houses, and are especially fond of the crowns of palm trees. The voice is a series of rather plaintive metallic squeaks.

114. PURPLE-BACKED STARLING (*Sturnus sturninus*) (7.5"/19cm)

Not as common as the previous species, this starling only visits Singapore during the northern winter. It is easily identified by the generally grey appearance and pale wing bars. Its habits are very similar to those of the Glossy Starling, although I have never seen it on the ground. Both species may be seen in mixed feeding flocks. It will join with other starlings in the evening roosts and when carrying out the display flights the pale rump is conspicuous. The White-shouldered Starling (*S. sinensis*) is very similar in appearance; it has a pale head and mantle, and more white in the wing, and is quite rare with only one or two recorded each year, but when present will mix with the other species of starlings.

ad.

113 imm.

114

JARVIS.

143

115. WHITE-VENTED MYNA *(Acridotheres javanicus)* (10"/25cm)

A bird apparently introduced by man in 1920 as a by-product of the cage bird trade. It now outnumbers the bird we call the Common Myna by about two to one in most habitats. It is more common in the immediate vicinity of humans and from this it could be inferred that it is more of a scavenging species than the other. Both species nest in holes where a large untidy nest is constructed. Holes in the roof space of buildings are frequently used, but natural sites include the crowns of palm trees where it nests at the base of the fronds or behind bunches of coconuts. Large communal roosts are formed in conjunction with starlings and Common Mynas. Before going to roost it can be seen gathering on areas of short turf for a last feed of the afternoon. They also gather on short grass in large numbers after rainstorms where they feed upon those organisms which have been flooded out of their burrows. The voice is very similar to that of the Common Myna and I have never learned to differentiate the two. At a distance it is told from the Common Myna by the generally grey-black appearance and absence of the yellow skin ringing the eye.

116. CRESTED MYNA *(Acridotheres cristatellus)* (10.5"/27cm)

Not a common species, but one which looks as though it may become so in the future. A native of Indo-china it has been introduced to several cities by escapes from the cage bird trade. They are feral in Penang where they seem to behave in a similar manner to the other mynas. In Singapore they were first recorded as a pair in Bras Basah three years ago and have since been shown to be breeding on the university campus at Kent Ridge and also the Institute of Education at Bukit Timah. More recent records have been from Siglap and Changi. It is a bigger, blacker bird than the White-vented with a large tuft of feathers over the ivory beak. Whether it will compound the problems created by our other exotic mynas remains to be seen. Between them they serve as a useful warning against the indiscriminate introduction of exotic species into any country where they may proliferate and become a pest.

117. BLACK-WINGED MYNA *(Sturnus melanopterus)* (10.5"/27cm)

Not a widespread or common species but I include it to complete the Singapore myna saga. A native of Indonesia, it has been recorded several times over the years in Singapore as having been accidentally or deliberately released from caged birds. The only population to have survived is that on St. John's Island where around 50 of them can be seen. It seems to be a more arboreal species than other mynas which prefer to feed on the ground. If this is so any spread to the mainland may be checked by the Glossy Starling.

118. COMMON MYNA *(Acridotheres tristis)* (10"/25cm)

Another very familiar bird. It is a fairly recent arrival to Singapore, having spread southwards down the Malay Peninsula as the forests were cleared for towns and agriculture. It was first recorded here in 1936, and has flourished and become very common. It will scavenge when waste food is easily available but seems to be more dependent upon natural food than the White-vented Myna. It feeds mostly on the ground, taking various insects and their larvae out of short turf, but will also visit fruit trees when ripe and take nectar from Coral Trees *(Erythrina variegata)*. They join with White-vented Mynas in night-time communal roosts which form in dense foliage, often in the lee of a tall embankment or building. The formation of some of these roosts in shade trees in car-parks and housing estates makes them a source of complaint. Juveniles have a brown head rather than a glossy black one. Certain birds lose all their head-feathers during moult and at this time the yellow skin of the head — normally visible only in the bare patch around the eye — gives them a strange appearance. The voice is a variety of harsh cries and whistles; one common one, often repeated, is "cree-cree-cree, kaa-kaa-kaa-kaa-kaa", the last five notes at a higher pitch.

115

116

118

117

145

119. CRIMSON SUNBIRD (*Aethopyga siparaja*) (4.25"/11cm)

Of all our beautiful sunbirds the male of this species has to be the best. The forehead and tail are a shining purple, the breast, mantle and inner parts of the wings are crimson, it has a yellow rump and a metallic purple "moustache". The female is very dull by comparison and difficult to tell from that of the Purple-throated. It is not uncommon in Singapore and may be seen in the forest, agricultural areas and occasionally mangrove. Although Bucknill and Chasen reported it as frequenting gardens often, I have never seen it in this type of habitat and the habitats surrounding residential areas. This probably reflects a change in the management of gardens. It is said to be very fond of the flower of *Eugenia malaccensis* (*Jambu bol*). The nest is found near to the ground: I watched one building at Bukit Timah Hill and the nest was barely six inches above the ground on a steep bank. It was built into the fronds of a fallen rattan, the dead leaves of which were used for construction. Every two to three minutes she followed the same flight path into the forest to collect spiders' webs. The Latin name of this species was given by Raffles who based it on the Malay name of "*burong sepah raja*", *sepah* aptly recalling the brilliant juice of the betel.

120. PURPLE-THROATED SUNBIRD (*Nectarinia sperata*) (4"/10cm)

One of the less common of our sunbirds, but one which can be met with in the forest or more remote rural areas, seldom occurring in parks and gardens. Throughout much of its range it is predominantly a coastal bird, but in Singapore the reverse is true. It is a tiny bird, only a little bigger than a flowerpecker. It often appears completely black, but when the sun catches it the cap can shine like a bright green beacon. It has a shining blue back and upper wing whilst the mantle is a dark matt brown. Caution is required because the throat can have a coppery sheen to it which may result in confusion with the much larger Copper-throated Sunbird (*N. calcostetha*). Also the dark crimson belly invites confusion with the Crimson Sunbird. The female has a black tail. In the forest I have seen it several times feeding off the flowers of *Saraca thaipingensis*, and in our remaining rural areas off coconuts.

Identifying Female Sunbirds

	BROWN-THROATED	OLIVE-BACKED	CRIMSON	PURPLE-THROATED
SIZE	large	small	small	very small
TAIL	olive	very dark brown, white tip	olive	very dark brown
BELLY	yellowish-olive	bright yellow	olive	yellowish in centre
BEAK	pale horn, short, thick shallow curve	black, sharp sharp curve	pale horn even curve	black, flat near head turns at tip

119 ♀

♂

120 ♀

♂

JARVIS.

121. OLIVE-BACKED SUNBIRD
(*Nectarinia jugularis*) (4.5"/11cm)

This is the most common of our sunbirds and can be found in every habitat, with the exception of the denser forest. It is particularly common in gardens and around the coast. Unfortunately it is the least spectacular in appearance, the male merely being adorned with a metallic blue throat and forehead. The female has yellow underparts which are brighter than any of the other species, and a white tip to the tail. In silhouette the curve on the beak of this bird is greater than in any of the other species. The first plumage of immature birds is indistinguishable from that of the female. Juvenile males slowly acquire the blue throat and may often be seen with just a few blue feathers, or a thin blue streak down the throat. It will feed on the same species of plants as the Brown-throated plus the flowers of *Callistemon, Erythrina* and *Russelia*. The nest is often placed low down in bushes and trees and sometimes on verandas. I have a record of one building inside the bedroom of a large house and two of it building high up on the balconies of tower blocks, on the 8th and 16th floors respectively! The nest is the usual pendant form, with an overhanging porch at the entrance and the outside decorated in a wonderful manner with a great variety of lichens, dead leaves, seed cases, and even caterpillar frass.

122.   BROWN-THROATED SUNBIRD *(Anthreptes malacensis)*   (5.5"/14cm)

One of the two common garden sunbirds. All the sunbirds demand a close look because some of their feathers have a metallic sheen and the colours will change depending on the direction of the sun. The male has a yellow belly, brown throat, olive cheeks, and a prominent metallic-purple shoulder patch. The mantle is also metallic and changes from purple to green, depending upon the light. The female has yellowish-olive underparts and an olive back. They will feed off nectar and are particularly attracted to Canna, Hibiscus (*bunga raya*), and coconuts. The larger flowers are often "robbed" from the back by piercing the base of the flower. They build a pendant nest made of grass and spiders' webs and lined with *lallang* seeds, fairly high up in a tree which often contains the red "*kerengga*" ants (*Oecophylla smaragdina*). Unlike the American hummingbirds (which are quite unrelated but often confused with sunbirds), they cannot hover for long periods and require large amounts of insects in their diet. The song is series of "chip" notes separated by the occasional "wheet" on a higher scale — "chip-chip-chip-chip, wheet, chip-chip".

149

123. LITTLE SPIDERHUNTER
(Arachnothera longirostra)

(6.3"/16cm)

123 ♂

Although still nectarivores, the enormous beak of the spiderhunters immediately separates them from sunbirds. Unfortunately only this one species now survives in Singapore. It is a very shy bird and good views are difficult to obtain, despite the fact that it always stays low in the forest undergrowth. It has a whitish throat separated from the face by a grey "moustache". The male, like most male sunbirds, has a tuft of orange feathers under the wings, these are fluffed out when displaying to the female. Its presence is usually shown by an olive flash as the bird flies past, giving a sharp "chip" call, often alarmingly close to you. The song, given from a concealed perch, is a rather hysterical "whee-choo" given at the rate of one or two per second; this has a ventriloquial quality and is hard to locate. It builds its nest from dead leaves, grass and spiders' webs, stitched to the underside of a broad leaf with plant fibres, the nest being a long tunnel with the leaf as the roof. It often uses bananas, but in Singapore I have seen it also using *Simpoh Ayer (Dillenia suffruticosa)*. In Malaysia this bird is very fond of banana plantations, but in Singapore I have searched our few remaining such sites with no success and have never recorded it anywhere other than in the forest reserve. I am not sure how the name originated. I have seen them hovering in front of spiders' webs and I am sure they will eat them if given the chance. However, I am equally sure that other insects will feature strongly in the diet and I know that they will take nectar from suitable flowers.

124. ORANGE-BELLIED FLOWERPECKER
(Dicaeum trigonostigma)

(3.5"/9cm)

Flowerpeckers are smaller and more compact than sunbirds, with a short beak and tail. The Orange-bellied male has a grey throat, orange back and belly with slatey-blue head and wings. The female is all olive-green with an orange-yellow rump. This bird is usually encountered in the forest and occasionally in the more wooded rural areas. It is usually in the tree tops but seems passionately fond of the fruits of the Straits Rhododendron (*Melastoma malabathricum*) and will feed low on these bushes wherever they grow. Like most of this family they have a jerky flight and make a rather mechanical "tick, tick, tick, tick" as they fly, almost as though they had been wound up. The song is a high-pitched, metallic six-note trill, descending in scale. They are very common around the forest edge and clearings, particularly where the Public Utilities Board water pipes follow a cleared path in the forest.

124 ♂

♀

JARVIS.

125 ♂

♀

JARVIS.

125. SCARLET-BACKED FLOWERPECKER
(*Dicaeum cruentatum*) (3.5"/9cm)

Although this bird may be encountered around the forest edge it is more common in open country, parks and gardens. Like its forest equivalent, the Orange-bellied, it is mainly a canopy bird and flits from tree-top to tree-top making the same mechanical ticking noise. Flowerpeckers will take nectar and small insects and it is difficult to know which is on the menu when they are probing at flowers. However fruit makes up a large part of the diet and this bird seems to make a specialty out of the fruits of the mistletoe species which grow freely in Singapore. Mistletoes are parasites on other trees and wherever one is in fruit this bird can be found; it can also be seen investigating those plants which are not fruiting. The seeds are very sticky and the birds must actively rub them against a branch to remove them when they are voided. In this way the flowerpecker is responsible for dispersing the seeds to new hosts. It is one of the finest looking of our garden birds, but good views may be difficult to obtain since it is constantly on the move. Its song produces some of the highest notes of any bird, consisting of a sharper version of the flight call immediately followed by a squeaking "chit-de-dee-de", reminiscent of two pieces of glass being rubbed together. I have never seen the nest in the field but have examined museum specimens which are the most exquisite structures, a purse-shaped pendant of *lallang* seeds and kapok bound with spider webs and fibres, usually high up under a clump of leaves.

126

126. EURASIAN TREE SPARROW (*Passer montanus*) (5.75"/15cm)

The somewhat confusing name of this bird reflects its habits in Europe where it is a woodland bird; near to habitation its place is taken by the very common House Sparrow (*Passer domesticus*). The House Sparrow has not yet invaded our corner of South-east Asia, but its role in scavenging around our dwellings is taken by the Eurasian Tree Sparrow. It seems likely that this is another species introduced by man's activities, but probably long before anyone was documenting bird movements. The main food item is grass seed but they seem capable of finding food in the most unlikely places. They will nest in any convenient hole, either in a tree, roof-space or ventilation holes of a house. Their constant presence and incessant chattering are so familiar that they are usually overlooked by most people.

153

127. BAYA WEAVER *(Ploceus philippinus)* (6"/15cm)

This bird is entirely dependent upon areas of long grass because it eats the seeds and constructs its woven nest from the blades. Thus it is confined entirely to the agricultural areas of Singapore, especially where there are coconuts. For reasons I have not been able to establish, in Singapore it seems to restrict its choice of nesting tree to coconuts. This restriction does not seem to hold elsewhere. In breeding plumage the male is a striking bird with black mask and bright yellow crown, however the female is a rather drab brown-streaked creature. The nest is a work of both art and engineering. Constructed as a pendant flask of woven grass, it has a long tube hanging below which leads into the side entrance. They are colonial, so anything up to 20 or 30 nests may be found together in one tree. Within these colonies half completed nests in the form of a "helmet" may be seen. The birds are polygamous and the male begins the breeding season by building two of the helmet stage nests. He then displays on them and tries to attract a female to mate with him. Presumably the quality of the contruction of the helmet helps the female to choose a male capable of building a good nest. The nests will often fall during storms and so the quality of construction is probably very important. Once paired the male then continues to build on one of the helmets until the nest is completed. The eggs are laid, and whilst the female is occupied with incubation and care of the young, the male builds another helmet and tries to attract another female. If he is successful the process is repeated. In this way the male always has one helmet spare, ready to mate with any available female. Usually a male only has two females, occasionally three. The male will defend the immediate vicinity of his nest against any intruding males. They have been recorded sharing trees with hornets' nests and also *"kerengga"* ants (although not in Singapore), which presumably provide some extra protection. The song is a wheezing rattle — "chit-chit-chit-chee-ee-ee-ee".

♂

♀

JARVIS.

154

completed
nest

helmet stage
nest

128. JAVAN MUNIA *(Lonchura leucogastroides)* (4.5"/11cm)

This species was introduced to Singapore from Indonesia in the early 1920s. It has thrived and is now probably our commonest munia. Like all munias it feeds on the seeds of grasses and bamboo. In the breeding season it seems to occur mostly in family parties, but at other times of the year flocks of 10 to 15 birds are usually seen. Part of its success seems to be attributable to its ability to feed on the seeds of lawn grasses (Bermuda Grass, Buffalo Grass etc.) where the seed heads may be found very close to the ground. It can be found in every habitat in Singapore, although in the nature reserve it is confined to the open areas around the dams and roadways. It is easily told from our other munias by the sharp line dividing the white belly from the brown breast. The White-bellied Munia found in Malaysia is similar but does not have a sharp dividing line and has brown sides and flanks.

129. SCALY-BREASTED MUNIA *(Lonchura punctulata)* (4.5"/11cm)

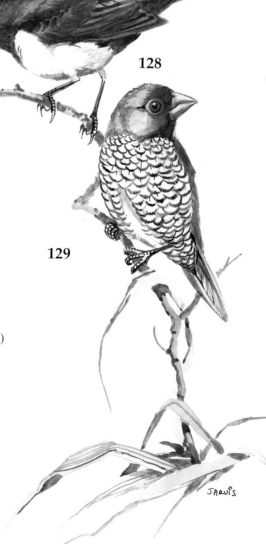

A very common member of this family, found in all habitats in Singapore, but especially common in the rural and agricultural areas where large flocks may form. This bird is absent from the very earliest collections in the region, and it is possible that this may also have been introduced to this region, at an earlier time than the Javan Munia. The back of the bird is a lighter brown than the Javan Munia and the white breast feathers are edged with brown, giving a beautiful scalloped appearance. The nest is an untidy ball of grass and bamboo leaves with a side entrance. It is placed in a bush about six to 20 feet above the ground; these bushes are often thorny. At the Botanic Gardens we had several pairs which nested in the crown of a *Ficus irregularis* near the lake. The nests were interspersed with those of the red *"kerengga"* ants (*Oecophylla smaragdina*), which did not trouble the birds and presumably provided protection.

130. WHITE-HEADED MUNIA
(Lonchura maja) (4.5"/11cm)

This bird is not too uncommon in Singapore, although it rarely occurs in parks and gardens and is usually met with in rural areas. It seems to be able to invade land which has been cleared for development and has become overgrown with wild grasses. Thus some of the largest flocks I have encountered (100) have been on or near to areas of reclaimed land: a very useful adaptation for a bird of Singapore. Immature munias are usually just various shades of buff all over and can be difficult to identify satisfactorily; the wisest thing is to try and locate the adults which are usually nearby.

131. CHESTNUT MUNIA *(Lonchura malacca)* (4.5"/11cm)

For fairly obvious reasons this is also known as the Black-headed Munia. It is probably the least common of our munias and is seen only in those areas with stands of long grass. Thus it is usually met with in places like Kranji reservoir and certain of the rural areas. I have never seen it in large flocks in Singapore: it is usually in ones or twos, mixed with a flock of other species of munia. In flight they give a small "preep" call which, coupled with the bouncy flight pattern of munias, gives the impression of a child's battery-driven toy! The nest is a ball of dried grasses usually built close to the ground in long grass or low bushes.

130

131

JARVIS.

NOMENCLATURE

Although it sounds a simple matter, bird names can pose several problems. The same species may occur in several different countries and be known by a different name in each one. Even in one region the name attached to a bird may slowly change as years go by and different books are written.

This has definitely been the case in South-east Asia where almost each successive author of the older books has used his own particular group of names. In an attempt to introduce some consistency the English names used in this book adhere to those used by King et al in *A Field Guide to the Birds of South-east Asia*.

English, or common, names are really just useful labels which we attach to a bird to identify it. The Latin or scientific names have deeper significance because they tell us about the relationships between birds. A glance through the checklist at the end of this book will reveal that the birds are grouped into *families*. All the Latin names of families end in *-dae*. Within the families each bird is given two Latin names, the first is the *genus* and the second the *species*. The generic names are the same for those species which are most closely related within the family. In some instances species with a wide geographical distribution show slight differences in features across their range; they are often then accorded a third name to identify the different race or sub-species. I have not identified the sub-species names of most of the birds unless it has some special significance in the Singapore context, for example in the Brown Shrike and Yellow Wagtail.

Because our knowledge of the relationships between birds is imperfect the Latin names continue to evolve as new advances are made. However, it would be nice to think that the English names have now stabilised to try and reduce the confusion which presently exists.

TECHNICAL NOTES

In zoogeographical terms Singapore is indistinguishable from the large peninsula of land immediately to its north. This peninsula has been dealt with in other texts of the region as the Malay Peninsula and comprises that land south of the Isthmus of Kra at 10° north. It includes the southern states of Thailand and the whole of West (Peninsular) Malaysia. This is the land mass referred to as "the peninsula" in the text whenever reference is made to the status of a bird in the surrounding region.

Singapore has only little distinction between climatic seasons but the status of many birds recorded here depends upon the seasons in the north temperate zone. Thus a "winter visitor" is that bird which visits Singapore from approximately October to April. Likewise "summer plumage" is that plumage adopted during the northern breeding season, which is May through to September. "Spring" and "autumn" are the transition periods.

In the colour plates preceding, no effort has been made to standardise the sizes of the birds as shown. Within one plate, where several species are illustrated, sizes are in proportion. To compare the sizes of birds in different plates the reader should refer to the length of the birds which is given in brackets immediately after the English and Latin name.

DOING MORE AND FURTHER READING

The birds covered by the book will satisfy the beginner for a while. Later I hope it will encourage the now-more-experienced birdwatcher to go out and learn more. As stated earlier the company of other enthusiasts is an invaluable source of new information and this can be achieved via the Malayan Nature Society (Singapore Branch). The society has an active bird group which organises outings and other activities. For further details contact: The Secretary, Malayan Nature Society, Botany Department, National University of Singapore, Kent Ridge, Singapore 0511.

At the back of this book will be found a species checklist. Space limitations have meant that only about half of the species on the list are covered in this book. For the identification of the remainder the reader is referred to *A Field Guide to the Birds of Southeast Asia* by King, Woodcock and Dickinson (Collins).

The author is in the process of preparing for publication an Annotated Checklist of Birds of Singapore. This will not be an aid to identification, but will instead describe the status and distribution of every species ever recorded from Singapore.

The Malayan Nature Society publishes annual Bird Reports in the Malayan Nature Journal. These cover peninsular Malaysia and Singapore and are compiled from observations submitted to Dr. D.R. Wells, Zoology Dept, University of Malaya, 59100 Kuala Lumpur. Submissions for this are always welcomed, especially from visitors whose observations may otherwise go unrecorded.

More information on the ecology, status and distribution of all species currently in Singapore can be found in the *Birds of the Malay Peninsula — Volume 5: conclusion, and survey of every species* by Lord Medway and D.R. Wells (published by H.F. and G. Witherby and University of Malaya Press).

The Oriental Bird Club is a society based in Britain but with a membership throughout this region. It publishes a twice-yearly bulletin and a journal, The Forktail. Membership fees are low and the contact address is:

The Oriental Bird Club, c/o The Lodge, Sandy, Bedfordshire SG19 2 DL, United Kingdom.

For those interested in learning more about the songs and calls of the birds of this region the Malayan Nature Society (address above) has three 45-minute cassettes of Malaysian bird songs and calls recorded by Rob Steubing for sale. There is also a *Field Guide to the Bird Songs of South-east Asia* by T. C. White, available from the British Library, National Sound Archives, 29 Exhibition Road, London SW7 2AS, England.

CHECKLIST OF THE BIRDS OF SINGAPORE

In the following checklist the status of each species is indicated by letters following the name:

R = resident
M = migrant
W = winter visitor
E = escape or feral species
C = common
U = uncommon (seen every year, but in small numbers)
Rr = rare (not recorded in every year)
V = vagrant (occurrence is unpredictable)

Procellariidae: SHEARWATERS
1. Streaked Shearwater (*Calonectris leucomelas*) V

Hydrobatidae: STORM PETRELS
2. Swinhoe's Storm Petrel (*Oceanodroma monorhis*) W

Sulidae: BOOBIES
3. Brown Booby (*Sula leucogaster*) V

Fregatidae: FRIGATEBIRDS
4. Christmas Frigatebird (*Fregata andrewsi*) V
5. Lesser Frigatebird (*Fregata ariel*) V

Ardeidae: HERONS, EGRETS, BITTERNS
6. Great-billed Heron (*Ardea sumatrana*) UR
7. Grey Heron (*Ardea cinerea*) CR
8. Purple Heron (*Ardea purpurea*) CR
9. Little Heron (*Butorides striatus*) CR
10. Chinese Pond-heron (*Ardeola bacchus*) UW
11. Cattle Egret (*Bubulcus ibis*) UW
12. Pacific Reef-egret (*Egretta sacra*) UR
13. Chinese Egret (*Egretta eulophotes*) RrW
14. Great Egret (*Egretta alba*) CW
15. Plumed Egret (*Egretta intermedia*) RrW
16. Little Egret (*Egretta garzetta*) CW
17. Black-crowned Night-heron (*Nycticorax nycticorax*) UR

18. Malayan Night-heron (*Gorsachius melanolophus*) RrW
19. Yellow Bittern (*Ixobrychus sinensis*) UR/CW
20. Schrenck's Bittern (*Ixobrychus eurhythmus*) UW
21. Cinnamon Bittern (*Ixobrychus cinnamomeus*) UR
22. Black Bittern (*Ixobrychus flaviocollis*) UW

Threskiornithidae: IBISES
23. Glossy Ibis (*Plegadis falcinellus*) V

Anatidae: DUCKS
24. Lesser Treeduck (*Dendrocygna javanica*) UW
25. Common Pintail (*Anas acuta*) RrW
26. Common Teal (*Anas crecca*) RrW
27. Garganey (*Anas querquedula*) UW
28. Northern Shoveler (*Anas clypeata*) RrW
29. Cotton Pygmy Goose (*Nettapus coromandelianus*) RrW

Pandionidae: OSPREY
30. Osprey (*Pandion haliaetus*) CW

Accipitridae: KITES, HAWKS, EAGLES
31. Black Baza (*Aviceda leuphotes*) CW
32. Eurasian Honey-buzzard (*Pernis apivorus*) CM
33. Bat Hawk (*Macheirhamphus alcinus*) V

34. Black-shouldered Kite (*Elanus caeruleus*) UR
35. Black Kite (*Milvus migrans*) UW
36. Brahminy Kite (*Haliastur indus*) CR
37. White-bellied Sea-eagle (*Haliaeetus leucogaster*) CR
38. Grey-headed Fish-eagle (*Icthyophaga icthyaetus*) V
39. Short-toed Eagle (*Circaetus gallicus*) RrM
40. Crested Serpent-eagle (*Spilornis cheela*) V
41. Marsh Harrier (*Circus aeruginosus*) UW
42. Pied Harrier (*Circus melanoleucos*) RrW
43. Japanese Sparrowhawk (*Accipiter gularis*) CW
44. Chinese Goshawk (*Accipiter soloensis*) RrM
45. Grey-faced Buzzard (*Butastur indicus*) RrM
46. Common Buzzard (*Buteo buteo*) V
47. Greater Spotted Eagle (*Aquila clanga*) UW
48. Rufous-bellied Eagle (*Hieraaetus kienerii*) V
49. Changeable Hawk-eagle (*Spizaetus cirrhatus*) UR
50. Black-thighed Falconet (*Microhierax fringillarius*) V
51. Eurasian Kestrel (*Falco tinnunculus*) RrW
52. Peregrine Falcon (*Falco peregrinus*) UW

Phasianidae: QUAIL
53. Blue-breasted Quail (*Coturnix chinensis*) UR

Turnicidae: BUTTONQUAIL
54. Barred Buttonquail (*Turnix suscitator*) UR

Rallidae: RAILS, CRAKES, COOT
55. Slaty-breasted Rail (*Rallus striatus*) CR
56. Red-legged Crake (*Rallina fasciata*) RrR
57. Baillon's Crake (*Porzana pusilla*) UW
58. Ruddy-breasted Crake (*Porzana fusca*) UR
59. White-browed Crake (*Porzana cinerea*) UR
60. White-breasted Waterhen (*Amaurornis phoenicurus*) CR
61. Watercock (*Gallicrex cinerea*) UW
62. Common Moorhen (*Gallinula chloropus*) UR
63. Purple Swamphen (*Porphyrio porphyrio*) UR
64. Common Coot (*Fulica atra*) V

Jacanidae: JACANAS
65. Pheasant-tailed Jacana (*Hydrophasianus chirurgus*) RrW

Rostratulidae: PAINTEDSNIPE
66. Greater Paintedsnipe (*Rostratula benghalensis*) UR

Charadriidae: PLOVERS
67. Grey-headed Lapwing (*Vanellus cinereus*) V
68. Red-wattled Lapwing (*Vanellus indicus*) V
69. Grey Plover (*Pluvialis squatarola*) CW
70. Pacific Golden Plover (*Pluvialis fulva*) CW
71. Common Ringed Plover (*Charadrius hiaticula*) RrM
72. Little Ringed Plover (*Charadrius dubius*) CW
73. Kentish Plover (*Charadrius alexandrinus*) UW
74. Malaysian Plover (*Charadrius peronii*) UW
75. Mongolian Plover (*Charadrius mongolus*) CW
76. Greater Sand-plover (*Charadrius leschenaultii*) UW
77. Oriental Plover (*Charadrius veredus*) RrW

Scolopacidae: CURLEWS, GODWITS, SANDPIPERS, SNIPE
78. Eurasian Curlew (*Numenius arquata*) UW
79. Whimbrel (*Numenius phaeopus*) CW
80. Eastern Curlew (*Numenius madagascariensis*) RrM
81. Black-tailed Godwit (*Limosa limosa*) CW
82. Bar-tailed Godwit (*Limosa lapponica*) UW
83. Spotted Redshank (*Tringa erythropus*) RrW
84. Common Redshank (*Tringa totanus*) CW
85. Marsh Sandpiper (*Tringa stagnatilis*) CW
86. Common Greenshank (*Tringa nebularia*) CW
87. Nordmann's Greenshank (*Tringa guttifer*) RrW
88. Green Sandpiper (*Tringa ochropus*) RrW
89. Wood Sandpiper (*Tringa glareola*) CW
90. Terek Sandpiper (*Xenus cinereus*) CW
91. Common Sandpiper (*Actitis hypoleucos*) CW

92. Grey-tailed Tattler (*Heteroscelus brevipes*) RrM
93. Ruddy Turnstone (*Arenaria interpres*) UW
94. Asian Dowitcher (*Limnodromus semipalmatus*) RrM
95. Pintail Snipe (*Gallinago stenura*)CW
96. Common Snipe (*Gallinago gallinago*) UW
97. Eurasian Woodcock (*Scolopax rusticola*) V
98. Red Knot (*Calidris canutus*) RrM
99. Great Knot (*Calidris tenuirostris*) UM
100. Rufous-necked Stint (*Calidris ruficollis*) CW
101. Temminck's Stint (*Calidris temminckii*) RrW
102. Long-toed Stint (*Calidris subminuta*) CW
103. Sharp-tailed Sandpiper (*Calidris acuminata*) RrM
104. Dunlin (*Calidris alpina*) RrM
105. Curlew Sandpiper (*Calidris ferruginea*) CW
106. Sanderling (*Calidris alba*) CW
107. Spoon-billed Sandpiper (*Eurynorhynchus pygmaeus*) RrM
108. Broad-billed Sandpiper (*Limicola falcinellus*) UM
109. Ruff (*Philomachus pugnax*) UM

Recurvirostridae: STILTS
110. Black-winged Stilt (*Himantopus himantopus*) RrM

Burhinidae: THICK-KNEES
111. Great Thick-knee (*Esacus magnirostris*) RrR

Glareolidae: PRATINCOLES
112. Oriental Pratincole (*Glareola maldivarum*) UM

Laridae: GULLS, TERNS
113. Common Black-headed Gull (*Larus ridibundus*) RrW
114. Brown-headed Gull (*Larus brunnicephalus*) RrW
115. White-winged Tern (*Chlidonias leucopterus*) CW
116. Gull-billed Tern (*Gelochelidon nilotica*) UM
117. Caspian Tern (*Hydroprogne caspia*) RrM
118. Common Tern (*Sterna hirundo*) UM
119. Black-naped Tern (*Sterna sumatrana*) UR
120. Bridled Tern (*Sterna anaethetus*) RrW
121. Little Tern (*Sterna albifrons*) CW
122. Great Crested Tern (*Sterna bergii*) CW
123. Lesser Crested Tern (*Sterna bengalensis*) UW

Columbidae: PIGEONS, DOVES
124. Thick-billed Pigeon (*Treron curvirostra*) V
125. Little Green Pigeon (*Treron olax*) V
126. Pink-necked Pigeon (*Treron vernans*) CR
127. Jambu Fruit-dove (*Ptilinopus jambu*) V
128. Feral Pigeon (*Columba livia*) CR
129. Red Turtle-dove (*Streptopelia tranquebarica*) E
130. Spotted Dove (*Streptopelia chinensis*) CR
131. Peaceful Dove (*Geopelia striata*) CR
132. Green-winged Pigeon (*Chalcophaps indica*) UR

Psittacidae: PARROTS
133. Rose-ringed Parakeet (*Psittacula krameri*) E
134. Red-breasted Parakeet (*Psittacula alexandri*) E
135. Long-tailed Parakeet (*Psittacula longicauda*) CR
136. Blue-rumped Parrot (*Psittinus cyanurus*) V
137. Blue-crowned Hanging Parrot (*Loriculus galgulus*) UR
138. Lesser Sulphur-crested Cockatoo (*Cacatua sulphurea*) E
139. Little Corella (*Cacatua sanguinea*) E

Cuculidae: CUCKOOS
140. Chestnut-winged Cuckoo (*Clamator coromandus*) UM
141. Large Hawk-cuckoo (*Cuculus sparverioides*) RrM
142. Hodgsons Hawk-cuckoo (*Cuculus fugax*) UM
143. Indian Cuckoo (*Cuculus micropterus*) UW
144. Banded Bay Cuckoo (*Cuculus sonneratii*) UR
145. Plaintive Cuckoo (*Cuculus merulinus*) UR
146. Brush Cuckoo (*Cacomantis variolosus*) V
147. Violet Cuckoo (*Chrysococcyx xanthorhynchus*) UR
148. Horsfield's Bronze Cuckoo (*Chrysococcyx basalis*) RrM
149. Malayan Bronze Cuckoo (*Chrysococcyx minutillus*) UR
150. Drongo Cuckoo (*Surniculus lugubris*) UR
151. Common Koel (*Eudynamys scolopacea*) UW
152. Chestnut-bellied Malkoha (*Phaenicophaeus sumatranus*) UR
153. Greater Coucal (*Centropus sinensis*) CR

154. Lesser Coucal (*Centropus bengalensis*) CR

Strigiformes: OWLS
155. Barn Owl (*Tyto alba*) UR
156. Collared Scops Owl (*Otus bakkamoena*) CR
157. Buffy Fish-owl (*Ketupa ketupu*) RrR/V
158. Brown Hawk-owl (*Ninox scutulata*) CR
159. Spotted Wood-owl (*Strix seloputo*) RrR

Caprimulgidae: NIGHTJARS
160. Malaysian Eared Nightjar (*Eurostopodus temminckii*) UR
161. Large-tailed Nightjar (*Caprimulgus macrurus*) CR

Apodidae: SWIFTS
162. Edible-nest Swiftlet (*Aerodramus fuciphagus*) CR
163. Black-nest Swiftlet (*Aerodramus maximus*) CR
164. White-bellied Swiftlet (*Collocalia esculenta*) V
165. White-vented Needletail (*Hirundapus cochinchinensis*) RrM
166. Brown Needletail (*Hirundapus giganteus*) UM
167. Fork-tailed Swift (*Apus pacificus*) CM
168. House Swift (*Apus affinis*) CR
169. Asian Palm-swift (*Cypsiurus balasiensis*) CR

Hemiprocnidae: TREESWIFTS
170. Grey-rumped Treeswift (*Hemiprocne longipennis*) CR
171. Whiskered Treeswift (*Hemiprocne comata*) V

Alcedinidae: KINGFISHERS
172. Common Kingfisher (*Alcedo atthis*) CW
173. Blue-eared Kingfisher (*Alcedo meninting*) V
174. Black-backed Kingfisher (*Ceyx erithacus*) V
175. Stork-billed Kingfisher (*Halcyon capensis*) UR
176. Ruddy Kingfisher (*Halcyon coromanda*) RrR
177. White-throated Kingfisher (*Halcyon smyrnensis*) CR
178. Black-capped Kingfisher (*Halcyon pileata*) CW
179. Collared Kingfisher (*Halcyon chloris*) CR

Meropidae: BEE-EATERS
180. Blue-tailed Bee-eater (*Merops philippinus*) CW

181. Blue-throated Bee-eater (*Merops viridis*) CR

Coraciidae: ROLLERS
182. Dollarbird (*Eurystomus orientalis*) CW, RrR

Capitonidae: BARBETS
183. Red-crowned Barbet (*Megalaima rafflesii*) UR
184. Coppersmith Barbet (*Megalaima haemacephala*) UR

Picidae: WOODPECKERS
185. Rufous Woodpecker (*Celeus brachyurus*) UR
186. Laced Woodpecker (*Picus vittatus*) CR
187. Crimson-winged Woodpecker (*Picus puniceus*) RrR
188. Banded Woodpecker (*Picus miniaceus*) CR
189. Common Goldenback (*Dinopium javanense*) UR
190. Great Slaty Woodpecker (*Mulleripicus pulverulentus*) V
191. White-bellied Woodpecker (*Dryocopus javensis*) RrR
192. Brown-capped Woodpecker (*Picoides moluccensis*) CR

Pittidae: PITTAS
193. Blue-winged Pitta (*Pitta moluccensis*) RrM
194. Mangrove Pitta (*Pitta megarhyncha*) RrR
195. Hooded Pitta (*Pitta sordida*) RrM

Hirundinidae: SWALLOWS
196. Sand Martin (*Riparia riparia*) UM
197. Barn Swallow (*Hirundo rustica*) CW
198. Pacific Swallow (*Hirundo tahitica*) CR
199. Red-rumped Swallow (*Hirundo daurica*) UM
200. Asian House Martin (*Delichon dasypus*) UM

Campephagidae: CUCKOO-SHRIKES, MINIVETS
201. Pied Triller (*Lalage nigra*) CR
202. Ashy Minivet (*Pericrocotus divaricatus*) CW
203. Scarlet Minivet (*Pericrocotus flammeus*) RrR

Chloropseidae: IORAS, LEAFBIRDS
204. Common Iora (*Aegithina tiphia*) CR
205. Greater Green Leafbird (*Chloropsis sonneratii*) V
206. Blue-winged Leafbird (*Chloropsis cochinchinensis*) RrR

Pycnonotidae: BULBULS

207. Straw-headed Bulbul (*Pycnonotus zeylanicus*) RrR
208. Black-headed Bulbul (*Pycnonotus atriceps*) UR
209. Red-whiskered Bulbul (*Pycnonotus jocosus*) E
210. Sooty-headed Bulbul (*Pycnonotus aurigaster*) E
211. Yellow-vented Bulbul (*Pycnonotus goiavier*) CR
212. Olive-winged Bulbul (*Pycnonotus plumosus*) CR
213. Cream-vented Bulbul (*Pycnonotus simplex*) CR
214. Red-eyed Bulbul (*Pycnonotus brunneus*) RrR
215. Ashy Bulbul (*Hypsipetes flavala*) V

Dicruridae: DRONGOS

216. Black Drongo (*Dicrurus macrocercus*) UW
217. Ashy Drongo (*Dicrurus leucophaeus*) V
218. Crow-billed Drongo (*Dicrurus annectans*) RrW
219. Greater Racket-tailed Drongo (*Dicrurus paradiseus*) CR

Oriolidae: OLD WORLD ORIOLES, FAIRY-BLUEBIRDS

220. Black-naped Oriole (*Oriolus chinensis*) CR
221. Asian Fairy-bluebird (*Irena puella*) UR

Corvidae: CROWS

222. House Crow (*Corvus splendens*) CR
223. Large-billed Crow (*Corvus macrorhynchos*) CR

Timaliidae: BABBLERS

224. Short-tailed Babbler (*Trichastoma malaccense*) CR
225. White-chested Babbler (*Trichastoma rostratum*) RrR
226. Abbott's Babbler (*Trischastoma abbotti*) UR
227. Moustached Babbler (*Malacopteron magnirostre*) RrR
228. Chestnut-winged Babbler (*Stachyris erythroptera*) CR
229. Striped Tit-babbler (*Macronous gularis*) CR
230. Hwamei (*Garrulax canorus*) E

Turdidae: THRUSHES

231. Siberian Blue Robin (*Erithacus cyane*) UM
232. Magpie Robin (*Copsychus saularis*) R
233. White-rumped Shama (*Copsychus malabaricus*) RrR/E
234. Stonechat (*Saxicola torquata*) UW
235. Eye-browed Thrush (*Turdus obscurus*) UM

Sylviidae: OLD WORLD WARBLERS

236. Flyeater (*Gerygone sulphurea*) CR
237. Inornate Warbler (*Phylloscopus inornatus*) RrM
238. Arctic Warbler (*Phylloscopus borealis*) CW
239. Eastern Crowned Warbler (*Phylloscopus coronatus*) UM
240. Great Reed-warbler (*Acrocephalus orientalis*) CW
241. Black-browed Reed-warbler (*Acrocephalus bistrigiceps*) UW
242. Pallas's Warbler (*Locustella certhiola*) UW
243. Lanceolated Warbler (*Locustella lanceolata*) UM
244. Common Tailorbird (*Orthotomus sutorius*) CR
245. Dark-necked Tailorbird (*Orthotomus atrogularis*) CR
246. Ashy Tailorbird (*Orthotomus ruficeps*) CR
247. Rufous-tailed Tailorbird (*Orthotomus sericeus*) CR
248. Yellow-bellied Prinia (*Prinia flaviventris*) CR
249. Zitting Cisticola (*Cisticola juncidis*) CR

Muscicapidae: OLD WORLD FLYCATCHERS

250. Dark-sided Flycatcher (*Muscicapa sibirica*) UW
251. Asian Brown Flycatcher (*Muscicapa latirostris*) CW
252. Yellow-rumped Flycatcher (*Ficedula zanthopygia*) UM
253. Mugimaki Flycatcher (*Ficedula mugimaki*) UM
254. Blue-and-White Flycatcher (*Cyanoptila cyanomelana*) RrM
255. Mangrove Blue Flycatcher (*Cyornis rufigastra*) RrR
256. Pied Fantail (*Rhipidura javanica*)CR
257. Black-naped Monarch (*Hypothymis azurea*) RrR
258. Japanese Paradise-flycatcher (*Terpsiphone atrocaudata*) RrM
259. Asian Paradise-flycatcher (*Terpsiphone paradisi*) UM

Pachycephalidae: WHISTLERS

260. Mangrove Whistler (*Pachycephala cinerea*) UR

Motacillidae: WAGTAILS, PIPITS

261. White Wagtail (*Motacilla alba*) RrM
262. Grey Wagtail (*Motacilla cinerea*) RrM
263. Yellow Wagtail (*Motacilla flava*) CW

264. Forest Wagtail (*Dendronanthus indicus*) UW
265. Richard's Pipit (*Anthus novaeseelandiae*) CR
266. Red-throated Pipit (*Anthus cervinus*) RrM

Laniidae: SHRIKES
267. Brown Shrike (*Lanius cristatus*) CW
268. Tiger Shrike (*Lanius tigrinus*) UW
269. Long-tailed Shrike (*Lanius schach*) UR

Sturnidae: STARLINGS, MYNAS
270. Philippine Glossy Starling (*Aplonis panayensis*) CR
271. White-shouldered Starling (*Sturnus sinensis*) RrM
272. Purple-backed Starling (*Sturnus sturninus*) CW
273. Black-winged Myna (*Sturnus melanopterus*) E
274. Common Myna (*Acridotheres tristis*) CR
275. White-vented Myna (*Acridotheres javanicus*) CR
276. Crested Myna (*Acridotheres cristatellus*) E
277. Hill Myna (*Gracula religiosa*) UR

Nectariniidae: SUNBIRDS, SPIDERHUNTERS
278. Plain Sunbird (*Anthreptes simplex*) V
279. Brown-throated Sunbird (*Anthreptes malacensis*) CR
280. Purple-throated Sunbird (*Nectarinia sperata*) UR
281. Copper-throated Sunbird (*Nectarinia calcostetha*) RrR
282. Olive-backed Sunbird (*Nectarinia jugularis*) CR
283. Crimson Sunbird (*Aethopyga siparaja*) CR
284. Little Spiderhunter (*Arachnothera longirostra*) CR

Dicaeidae: FLOWERPECKERS
285. Orange-bellied Flowerpecker (*Dicaeum trigonostigma*) CR
286. Scarlet-backed Flowerpecker (*Dicaeum cruentatum*) CR

Ploceidae: SPARROWS, WEAVERS, MUNIAS
287. Eurasian Tree Sparrow (*Passer montanus*) CR
288. Baya Weaver (*Ploceus philippinus*) UR
289. Java Sparrow (*Padda oryzivora*) E
290. White-rumped Munia (*Lonchura striata*) RrR
291. Javan Munia (*Lonchura leucogastroides*) E
292. Scaly-breasted Munia (*Lonchura punctulata*) CR
293. Chestnut Munia (*Lonchura malacca*) UR
294. White-headed Munia (*Lonchura maja*) UR

Fringillidae: FINCHES, BUNTINGS
295. Yellow-breasted Bunting (*Emberiza aureola*) RrM

BIBLIOGRAPHY

BUCKNILL, J.A.S., and CHASEN, F.N. 1927. *The Birds of Singapore Island.* Government Printing Office, Singapore.

GIBSON-HILL, C.A. 1950. *A Checklist of the Birds of Singapore Island.* Bull. Raffles Mus. 20:132-183.

GIBSON-HILL, C.A. 1950. *Ornithological Notes from the Raffles Museum: 23. Notices of four birds new to, or rare in, the Malay peninsula.* Bull. Raffles Mus. 20:180-186.

GLENISTER, A.G. 1951. *The Birds of the Malay Peninsula, Singapore and Penang.* Oxford University Press, London.

KING, B., WOODCOCK, M. and **DICKINSON, E.C.** 1975 *A Field Guide to the Birds of South-east Asia.* Collins, London.

LENTON, G.M. 1984. *The Feeding and Breeding Ecology of Barn Owls* (Tyto alba) *in Peninsular Malaysia.* Ibis 126:551-575.

MADOC, G.C. 1956. *An Introduction to Malayan Birds.* Malayan Nature Society, Kuala Lumpur.

MEDWAY, LORD and **WELLS, D.R.** 1976. *The Birds of the Malay Peninsula.* H.F. and G. Witherby and Univ. Malaya Press. Kuala Lumpur.

SMYTHIES, B.E. 1981. *The Birds of Borneo* (3rd ed.). Sabah Society and Malayan Nature Society, Kuala Lumpur.

GLOSSARY

Bars:	tranverse marks (usually dark) on the plumage
Cap:	the top part of the head incorporating the forehead, crown, upper nape and eyebrow
Carpal:	the "wrist" or point at which the wing bends backwards
Cheek:	the area of the face under the eye
Collar:	a band of colour in a ring (often incomplete) round the neck
Crest:	a tuft of feathers on the front or rear of the head
Diurnal:	active in the daytime
Ear-patch:	the feathers overlying the ear position (ear coverts)
Eyebrow:	a line of colour sweeping over the eye
Eye-stripe:	a line of colour running through the eye
Frugivorous:	eating fruit
Facial disk:	the rather flat, rounded appearances of an owl's face
Immature:	a young animal before reaching adulthood
Insectivorous:	eating insects
Kelong	a large, free-standing fish-trap made of tall poles standing in the sea
Lallang:	a common wasteland grass, *Imperata cylindrica*
Lappets:	a fleshy wattle usually on the head or neck
Mantle:	back, upper wing coverts and scapulars combined (see topography)
Montane:	inhabiting a mountain region
Morphs:	animals of different appearance belonging to the same species
Nasal:	concerning the nose, as in a sound uttered through the nose
Nectarivorous:	drinking nectar
Nocturnal:	active at night
Nuptial plumage:	the pattern of feathers adopted during the breeding season
Piscivorous:	eating fish
Plumage:	the covering of feathers
Polygamous:	having more than one mate
Raptor:	a diurnal bird of prey
Roost:	a perch or place for a sleeping bird, sometimes used as a collective term for a flock of sleeping birds
Shaft:	the stiff central rod of a feather, also called the rachis
Shield:	a hard horny plate from the base of the bill covering the forehead
Streak:	a longitudinal mark on the plumage
Vagrant:	a bird which occurs irregularly in an area.
Ventriloquial:	the impression that a sound comes from a place other than the source
Wing bar:	bands formed on the wing when the tips of the greater and/or median wing coverts are a different colour from their base

166

INDEX

NATURE SERIES

Kingfishers of the World

Polynesia
Birds of Tahiti
Underwater Guide to Tahiti
Insects of Hawai'i
Sharks of Hawai'i
Underwater Guide to Hawai'i
Plants and Flowers of Hawai'i

Tropical
Sharks of Tropical and Temperate Seas
Living Corals

Asia
Birds of Thailand
Underwater Guide to the South China Sea
Plants and Flowers of Singapore
Plants and Flowers of Malaysia
Orchids of Asia